Aesop's Keys to Profitable Marketing
Dr. Betsy Kruger
Publishing Directions
9781928782582 $17.95 www.betsykruger.com

Business leaders who look for more than the usual dry approach to marketing, who wonder whether the 80/20 rule is a proven fact, and who seek real-world applications of this cornerstone of business achievement will find *Aesop's Keys to Profitable Marketing* to be a vivid, essential discussion.

In fact, *Aesop's Keys* doesn't just sprinkle in real-world models to spice up theory: it centers upon some 24 examples that clearly show how to apply the 80/20 rule to various marketing decisions, explaining basics such as why quality beats quantity every time, when discounted pricing fails, and how to leverage limited resources by using suppliers.

Where other business books would approach marketing decisions with generalities, *Aesop's Keys* provides specifics; right down to tables that predict how much a narrow focus will magnify profits. For example, one marketing decision is to develop distribution channels that consistently "wow" customers in its target market.

Each business insight is cemented by a business-oriented vignette paired with an actual Aesop tale. In one tale, a businessman asks Aesop to evaluate a promotion for his business and Aesop mocks him for being "his own trumpeter." In contrast, effective promotions empathize with key customers, demonstrate value, and provide prospects with concrete and specific information. Business savvy about promotions is summarized with the *Aesop Key* to "trumpet empathy."

Key marketing strategies such as profiling preferred customers, adding value, and pruning unprofitable products or services are introduced and then applied at every step of the way. More than merely conveying the 80/20 rule, *Aesop's Keys* encourages business leaders to revise their marketing plans and effectively apply the 80/20 rule to various aspects of marketing their businesses.

All aspects have been covered elsewhere to some degree or another; but presenting them under one cover in a format that consistently and effectively cements theory with real-world marketing decisions makes *Aesop's Keys* a powerful standout in a genre replete with overly complex or poorly thought-out works.

The bottom line? Business leaders seeking profitable results through new, applied directions will find that *Aesop's Keys to Profitable Marketing* provides an easy formula of success for virtually any business endeavor, from running a health clinic to selling product.

D. Donovan, Senior Reviewer,
Midwest Book Review, Oregon, Wisconsin

Testimonies by Successful Entrepreneurs

"Marketing, and the whole firm, should devote extraordinary endeavor toward delighting, keeping forever, and expanding the sales of the 20% of customers who provide 80% of the firm's profits and cash. It can multiply the profitability of corporations and the effectiveness of any organization."

— **RICHARD KOCH**, CONSULTANT AND AUTHOR OF THE MILLION COPY BESTSELLER, *THE 80/20 PRINCIPLE: THE SECRET TO ACHIEVING MORE WITH LESS*, GIBRALTAR.

"Want to generate more profits? Dr. Kruger lays out easy-to-follow ways to increase your profits."

— **KEN BERNHARDT**, TAYLOR E. LITTLE REGENTS PROFESSOR OF MARKETING EMERITUS, ROBINSON COLLEGE OF BUSINESS, GEORGIA STATE UNIVERSITY, PAST PRESIDENT OF THE AMERICAN MARKETING ASSOCIATION, AND AUTHOR OF MARKETING TEXTBOOKS, WOODSTOCK, GEORGIA.

"During my years of selling and servicing insurance, the results were exactly as predicted in her book. Dr. Kruger has laid out an easy-to-use process for growing top customers of any business."

— **ROBERT IOCCO**, CPA, CIC, CEO, TRUSTPOINT INSURANCE, BRISTOL, VIRGINIA.

"I use the 80/20 rule to manage my chiropractic clinic—and my life. As a result, I attract and retain the best patients and accomplish more in less time."

— **DR. DAVID MALLORY**, NECK, BACK, AND HEADACHE RELIEF CENTER, DAYTONA BEACH, FLORIDA.

"Just as Dr. Kruger coached me, Holland Financial is focused on serving our target demographic. She mentors with a sharp perception of what really matters."

— **DAVID HOLLAND**, CEO, HOLLAND FINANCIAL INC.,
ORMOND BEACH, FLORIDA.

"Fun to read, yet full of inspiring examples on how to overcome obstacles and succeed. Kruger has really captured Aesop's spirit and what it means in today's world."

— **MIHALIS HALKIDES**, PH.D., DIRECTOR, INSTITUTE FOR APPLIED BUSINESS
STRATEGIES, BETHUNE-COOKMAN UNIVERSITY, DAYTONA BEACH, FLORIDA.

"I simply love the flow of Dr. Betsy Kruger's book—so profound yet so simple to follow. Every chapter leads to new decisions, which combined, become my strategic marketing plan."

— **DR. CONNIE SCHOTTKY**, SCHOTTKY AND OSTERHOLT
CONSULTANCY, LOS ANGELES, CALIFORNIA.

Aesop's Keys to Profitable Marketing

Dr. Betsy Kruger

Publishing Directions
PO Box 715
Avon, CT 06001-0715

First paperback edition 2015

For information about special discounts for bulk purchase or to bring the author to your live event, please contact Brian Jud, President, Premium Book Company at (860) 675-1344 or BrianJud@premiumbookcompany.com.

Cover and Interior design: 1106 Design

Editor: Eileen Albrizio, www.EileenAlbrizio.com, EileenRain@aol.com

Library of Congress Control Number: 2014910201

ISBN: 978-1-928782-58-2

Manufactured in the United States of America

10 9 8 7 6 5 4 3 2 1

Publisher's Cataloging-in-Publication
(Provided by Quality Books, Inc.)

Kruger, Elizabeth Rush.
    Aesop's keys to profitable marketing / by Dr. Betsy
Kruger. — First paperback edition.
    pages cm
    Includes bibliographical references and index.
    LCCN 2014910201
    ISBN 9781928782582

    1. Marketing—Management. 2. Entrepreneurship.
    3. Success in business. 4. Branding (Marketing)
    5. Aesop's fables—Adaptations.   I. Aesop. II. Title.

HF5415.13.K727 2015   658.8
                QBI14-1410

Table of Contents

Book Review   i

Testimonies   iii

Preface   xv

1. **Mission: How to Rule a Marketplace**   1
    Will a Lion Cub Rule as King?   3
    Key #1: Focus on Quality.   7

2. **Specialty: How to Specialize**   11
    Was a Peacock Blessed?   12
    Key #2: Compete on Strength.   19

3. **Suppliers: How to Avoid Weaknesses**   23
    Can a Mouse Save a Lion?   25
    Key #3: Delegate Weaknesses.   30

4. **Target Market: How to Describe Key Customers**   33
    Is Haste a Waste?   34
    Key #4: Describe Key Customers.   39

5. **Products and Services: How to Offer Benefits**   43
    When Is a Fox Hungry?   44
    Key #5: Offer Treasures.   49

6. **Pricing: How to Set Prices**   **53**
    What Saves an Apple Tree?   54
    Key #6: Price as Valued.   59

7. **Distribution: How to Build Loyalty**   **63**
    Why Did a Tortoise Beat a Hare?   64
    Key #7: Deliver Delight.   70

8. **Promotion: How to Promote**   **73**
    Who Believes a Conceited Ad?   74
    Key #8: Trumpet Empathy.   80

9. **Prospecting: How to Target Prospects**   **85**
    What Teaches a Crab?   86
    Key #9: Target Key Prospects.   91

10. **Customer Service: How to Set Policy**   **95**
    Can a Soldier Ride a Donkey?   96
    Key #10: Reward the Best.   99

11. **Budgeting: How to Allocate Money**   **105**
    What Use is a Miser's Gold?   106
    Key #11: Concentrate Resources.   107

12. **Taking Action: How to Spark Profits**   **115**
    What Proves the Truth?   118
    Key #12: Jump into Action.   121

Endnotes   **123**

Bibliography   **127**

Index   **131**

List of Figures

Figure 1: The 80/20 Rule   6

Figure 2: The Pareto Distribution   15

Figure 3: Results from Tasks   16

Figure 4: Profits from Delegating   27

Figure 5: Profits from Key Customers   36

Figure 6: The Pareto Distribution on a Log-Log Plot   37

Figure 7: Prune Products and Services   46

Figure 8: Deliver Delight   69

Figure 9: Empathetic Promotions   76

Figure 10: Describe Key Customers   88

Figure 11: Delight Key Customers   89

Figure 12: Convert Prospects Into Customers   89

Figure 13: Complainers   98

List of Tables

Table 1: Distribution of Hats   5

Table 2: An Example of the Theory of Comparative Advantage   28

Table 3: Steps in Pricing as Valued   57

Table 4: Steps in Targeting Key Prospects   90

Table 5: An Example of Sales Commissions   100

Table 6: Layers of the 80/20 Rule   119

This book is dedicated to my husband, Kenneth Henry Kruger. His love for me, for mankind, and for economic progress inspires my heartfelt gratitude.

Preface

Greetings Fellow Travelers.

We are all travelers on our path of life. On the path are entrepreneurs who grimly toil long hours for little profit. We see employees jogging in place, digging ever deeper the debt that shackles them to tedious jobs. Retired travelers fret because they have outlived their money. Off the path are unemployed travelers, exhausted from their job search. Does my friend Jamie remind you of someone who is waylaid on the path of life?

> Jamie paid for college by starting a business. After graduating and many years of employment, Jamie was fired. At first, Jamie searched for a suitable position.

> After two years of unemployment, Jamie became desperate to accept a job—any job. As time passed, Jamie's confidence wavered, savings vanished, and anguish deepened.

> I wonder why Jamie is still idling on the wayside of life, instead of resuming a successful business.

Do you recognize yourself as a fellow traveler? Do you feel stymied in your progress? Do you want to run a successful business? Do you want to prosper on your life's journey?

Fellow Travelers, you're in luck.

In your hands are keys to your progress. *Aesop's Keys to Profitable Marketing* shows you how to prosper by benefiting others. The book coaches you to describe, delight, and duplicate the key customers of your business. Embrace its content, apply it to your business, and profit from your marketing decisions.

The chapters open with an update of an Aesop tale that resonates with today's business leaders. Its wisdom relates to a key marketing decision. The 80/20 rule predicts the results of the decision, and business examples describe actual results. Each chapter closes by coaching you to use one of *Aesop's Keys to Profitable Marketing* in your business.

The book motivates you to focus your marketing decisions. You will begin by clarifying the mission, specialty, suppliers, and target market of your business. Then you will decide about its products and services and how to price, distribute, and promote them. You will finish with decisions about prospecting, customer service, budgeting, and taking action.

These twelve key marketing decisions encompass the components of a strategic marketing plan. When you complete this book, you will have a customized plan for profiting from the 80/20 rule. When you implement the plan, you and your business can prosper.

CHAPTER 1

Mission: How to Rule a Marketplace

A Mentor Reveals How to Spark Profits.

Early on a Monday morning, two independent distributors are enjoying lattes at Starbucks. The novice jests about her latest encounters and the mentor shares photos of her family's weekend jaunt.

After enjoying their rapport and lattes, her mentor asks, "How is your prospecting coming along?" Smugly, the novice heaves her list of prospects across the table. With a scornful toss of her hair, her mentor says, "I have only a few prospects."

The novice sips her latte and then asks, "Why do you have so few prospects? I contact lots of prospects, hoping a few will buy from me."

"I easily convert most of my prospects into customers."

After wincing, the novice says. "I work hard to convert a few prospects into customers."

"I can predict who will become customers and which ones will buy the high-priced items."

Dumbfounded, the novice gulps her latte and says, "My buyers threaten to switch to a lower-priced competitor. What's your secret?"

Building up the suspense, her mentor says, "Besides, I know who will continue to buy from me."

Muttering into her empty mug, the novice says, "I end up with a mess of complaints—and low commissions. Why don't you tell me your secret?"

"I can even predict who will become highly profitable customers. Unlike you, I consistently earn high commissions."

"I also want to work less and earn more."

Having piqued her interest, her mentor whispers in her ear, "Quality not quantity counts. Focus on high-quality prospects and your commissions will soar. Quality is the key to sparking your profits."

Eagerly, the novice asks, "But who are my high-quality prospects?"

"We're in different businesses, so my top prospects are different from yours." Her mentor opens her briefcase and gives her *Aesop's Keys to Profitable Marketing*. "This book will coach you to identify your high-quality prospects so you can be as successful as I am."

This vignette is similar to one of Aesop's fables. Many believe that a Greek slave named Aesop told tales in the sixth century BC on the island of Samos in the eastern Aegean Sea. Aesop's fables became popular. Soon lawyers were using Aesop's logic to argue cases and partygoers were sharing his humor with friends in the farthest reaches of the Greek Empire. The popularity of Aesop's tales spread throughout Western civilization and their wisdom still resonates in our lives today.[1]

Will a Lion Cub Rule as King?
An Aesop Tale

A vixen leads her litter of little foxes up to a lioness and sneers, "You only bore one cub."

Tossing her head in scorn, the lioness roars, "Only one, but he will rule as king of the animals."

Aesop noticed that quality produces better results than quantity. "Do not judge merit by quantity, but by worth. Quality not quantity counts."

Quality Beats Quantity.

Does quality really count?

The vixen bore a quantity of little foxes, but the lioness bore one high-quality cub. In modern jargon, a vixen is an ill-tempered and flirtatious woman; whereas a lioness is a woman who is exceptional at everything she does, from taking care of her family to running a business venture.

Aesop's tale about one princely lion cub and a litter of foxes conveys that quality is better than quantity. But businesses usually count the quantity, not the quality of their customers. Does quality count in your business? Do a few high-quality customers produce more profits than a large quantity of your other customers? Read on and you will discover why I know that your answer will be, "Yes."

I learn from my own seminar.

At my first seminar about this book, I boldly stated, "Let's test if quality counts more than quantity. Our inputs will be the people in this room and our outputs will be what? We'll pull them out of a hat. Just to be outlandish, they will be—hats. We'll see if a few people own most of the hats."

Explaining the test, I said, "We'll define 'high-quality' hat owners as possessing many hats and 'low-quality' hat owners as possessing few hats. We'll rank everyone in the room by how many hats they own. Will a few high-quality hat owners possess most of the hats and a large quantity of low-quality hat owners possess just a few hats? If so, then quality not quantity counts."

Starting off, I remarked, "I love to walk on the beach, play tennis, and ski, so I own a variety of hats—sun hats, tennis visors, and ski caps. I suppose I own about 15 hats."

I asked each person in the room to count their hats and a participant named Terry recorded their answers. Many people were low-quality hat owners since they owned no hat or only 1 hat. A few people were high-quality hat owners since they owned 2 or more hats. To my surprise, I was the highest quality hat owner in the room.

I was worried that our small sample would bias our results. Terry reported, "The 20 people in the room own 26 hats. The 4 who are high-quality hat owners own 21 hats so 20 percent own 81 percent of the hats. The 16 who are low-quality hat owners own 5 hats so 80 percent own 19 percent of the hats" *(Table 1)*.

Table 1: Distribution of Hats

	People	Hats
High quality hat owners	4 (20%)	21 (81%)
Low quality hat owners	16 (80%)	5 (19%)
Total	20	26

I said, "Quality not quantity counts for hats so we can conclude that quality does count." Terry said, "One person owns 15 hats." I said, "At least we're not counting shoes."

How Much Does Quality Count?

What is the 80/20 rule?

Aesop taught "quality not quantity counts," but two millennia later Pareto discovered just how much quality counts. Vilfredo Pareto was the Professor of Political Economy at the University of Lausanne in Switzerland. His brilliance attracted students from throughout Europe. Pareto taught them macroeconomics and advocated capitalism, free trade, and laissez-faire government.

In 1887, Vilfredo Pareto researched the effect of quality on results.[2] Pareto analyzed many types of data and discovered an amazing consistency. His students named this consistency the 80/20 rule.

The top 20 percent of the inputs produces 80 percent of the outputs, whereas the bottom 80 percent of the inputs produces only 20 percent of the outputs (*Figure 1*).

Figure 1: The 80/20 Rule

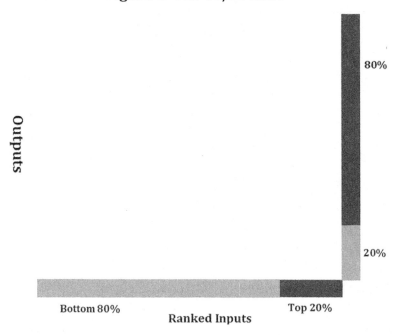

Does the 80/20 rule predict results?

Taking a leap of logic, Pareto assumed these results are predictable. Let's test whether the 80/20 rule is a universal law that predicts results. Just follow these three simple steps.

1. Rank at least 100 unbiased inputs in sequential order by the size of their outputs.

2. Identify the top 20 percent and bottom 80 percent of your inputs.

3. See if the top 20 percent of the inputs produced 80 percent of the outputs. If so, you have shown that the 80/20 rule is a universal law that predicts results.

For example, you can predict the most profitable 20 percent of your customers will produce 80 percent of your profits. This means these key customers will produce four-fold profits. Just imagine how much your business can profit from the 80/20 rule. The first key to profitable marketing is this.

Key #1: Focus on Quality.

How can your business rule its market like a regal lioness?

According to the 80/20 rule, a business that offers high-quality products and services will be more profitable than a business that offers low-quality items. The first step in focusing on quality is to revisit the mission of your business. Are you sure that your business offers high-quality products and services?

For example, we'll assume that you prefer doing what you do best. If you're great at carving statues, you love being a sculptor, or if you excel at managing construction, you love being a general contractor.

It's not a matter of trying harder, but trying less, and enjoying yourself more. What do you most enjoy doing in your free time? Allow yourself the freedom to discover what you do best.

More importantly, what does your business do best? What high-quality products and services can your business offer its customers? When your business offers high-quality items, its profits will greatly improve. Your business can rule your market like a regal lioness if your business offers high quality products and services.

"In the race for quality there is no finish line."
Doris Kearns [Goodwin], a Pulitzer Prize-winning
biographer of American presidents.

 ## Apply Key #1: The Mission of Your Business is to Focus on Quality.

Its mission should reflect what you do best.

Remembering your childhood, what did you most enjoy doing with your free time?

- Being with people

- Considering ideas

- Working with things and numbers

Which type of activity did you prefer?

- Analyzing
- Building
- Entertaining
- Exercising
- Harvesting

- Helping
- Managing
- Teaching
- Trading

What do you most enjoy doing now?

- Creating
- Fulfilling
- Leading

- Measuring
- Persuading
- Planning

What type of customers do you prefer?

- Consumers

- Businesses

- Government agencies

- Non-profit organizations

The mission of your business is to offer what high-quality products and services?

A successful man is a "Jack of all trades, but master of one."
Benjamin Franklin, a founding father of the United States,
scientist, inventor, author, and diplomat, 1706–1790.

CHAPTER 2

Specialty: How to Specialize

A Youth Discovers His Destiny.

A disheartened young man snoozes on a sofa, hugging his laptop. His girlfriend's ring tone wakes him and she says, "What's up?"

He whines, "Nothing and I'm going nowhere. I'm a college graduate, but no one wants to hire me—not even as a free intern. My parents laugh at me and I'm rotting in their basement with no way to escape."

His girlfriend interrupts his anguish. "My grandma wants to keep up with her grandchildren on Facebook. Will you teach her how to use Facebook?"

Brightening, he says, "Sure, I'll be glad to teach her. My rate is twenty-five dollars per hour. Does your grandma have friends?"

"Grandma has lots of friends who are eager to learn Facebook. You were awesome at teaching Facebook to my friends. You're blessed with this skill."

"Instead of searching desperately for a job, I'll create my own job and start a business. My destiny is to teach the older generation how to use Facebook."

She catches his excitement. "You'll go far by using your strength."

Was a Peacock Blessed?
An Aesop Tale

A peacock complains to a Greek goddess named Juno, "When I utter a sound, the other birds laugh at my ugly voice. I envy the nightingale's song."

Comforting him, the Greek goddess says, "Your neck flashes like an emerald and your tail is gorgeous. You're blessed in beauty, not in song."

"What good is beauty when my voice is so ugly?"

"I blessed every bird with a unique destiny." Juno chants, "The destiny of the nightingale is song, the eagle is strong, and so on. You alone are dissatisfied with your blessing. If I were to give you a lovely voice, you would quickly find another reason to complain!"

Aesop warns against jealousy. "You go further by using your own gift."

Know Thyself.

Was Aesop right?

Do you go further by using your own gift? Will the disheartened youth become a profitable entrepreneur? For example, Mark Zuckerberg's skill at website portfolios led to Facebook; Steve Jobs' skill at product design led to Apple; and Jeff Bezos' skill at Internet marketing led to Amazon.com. How far can your business go by using your own gift?

Learn from my weaknesses.

For several years, I managed projects for various marketing research providers. After a few months of employment, each company would abruptly fire me. I tried harder and harder to succeed, but they kept firing me. What was going on?

I tried so hard to succeed as a marketing researcher that I no longer knew myself. Marketing researchers excel at reporting facts so I kept assuring myself, "Of course, I'm technical, practical, objective, and orderly."

One way to "know thyself" is to identify your traits with the *Myers-Briggs Type Indicator*. This personality test contrasts four sets of traits: extraversion (E) versus introversion (I), intuition (N) versus sensation (S), thinking (T) versus feeling (F), and judging (J) versus perceiving (P).[3]

The *Myers-Briggs Type Indicator* revealed my core traits are opposite from what I expected. To my surprise, I'm extraverted, intuitive, subjective, and spontaneous, rather than introverted, sensory, thinking, and judging. I excel at solving problems, not reporting facts like a marketing researcher. I was specializing in my weaknesses, not in my strengths!

What is my strength?

Decades ago I discovered my greatest strength at a singles dance. A stranger asked, "Why don't you ask me to dance?" I said, "I never ask a man to dance and besides, you are fourteen years younger than I am." Surprised that I knew his age, he teased, "Do you also know my occupation?" I correctly guessed the man was a computer analyst.

Astonished, he walked me over to his two friends to guess their ages and occupations. I correctly guessed their ages and one was clearly a factory operative. The other one confused me. "I can't decide whether you are a manager or a mechanical engineer." No wonder I was confused—he managed mechanical engineers.

Sometimes I play an intuitive game when I travel by plane. With their consent, I guess the identity of passengers. For example, I correctly deduced a passenger was 28 years old, an expert in computer systems, and an employee of Arthur Anderson Consulting.

After confirming that he lacked a girlfriend, I said, "Now I'll guess what you do for fun." After a lengthy pause, I concluded, "You do nothing for fun. You just track your investments on the Internet." He cringed.

How Much Further Do You Go by Using Your Own Gift?

What is the Pareto distribution?

Pareto predicted the top 20 percent of a large unbiased sample of inputs will consistently produce 80 percent of the outputs, and vice versa. But Pareto was curious about the other inputs, so he related inputs to outputs on graph paper. He sequenced all inputs on the horizontal axis and accumulated their outputs on the vertical axis.

Whenever he related a large unbiased sample of inputs to outputs, the points traced the same concave curve that others called the Pareto distribution. See how *Figure 1* in the first chapter summarizes the Pareto distribution *(Figure 2)*.

Figure 2: The Pareto Distribution

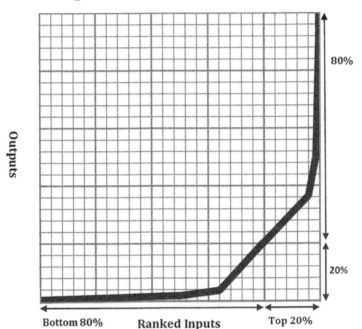

Does the Pareto distribution predict your results?

Let's consider the strengths and weaknesses of your business. For example, you can plot its tasks on the Pareto distribution and predict their profitability as follows.

1. Rank the tasks of your business in sequence by the profitability of their results.

2. Classify the top 20% as its strengths and the bottom 80% as its weaknesses.

15

3. Predict the top 20% of the tasks will produce 80% of your profits, thereby achieving 4-fold results (80%/20% = 4) *(Figure 3)*.

Figure 3: Results from Tasks

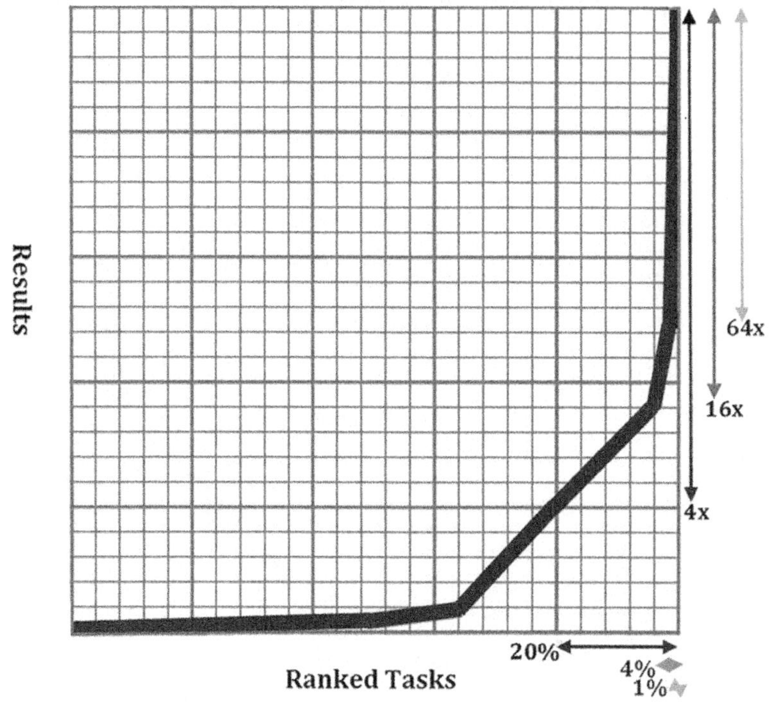

Let's gradually move upward and to the right on the Pareto distribution and predict even better results for your business.

- You will achieve 4-fold results from the top 20% of the tasks of your business.

- You will achieve 16 (4^2) results from the top 4% ($20\%^2$) of its tasks.

- You will achieve 64-fold (4^3) results from the top .8% ($20\%^3$) of its tasks.

- You will achieve 256-fold (4^4) results from the top .16% ($20\%^4$) of its tasks.

Aesop said, "You go further by using your own gift," and the Pareto distribution proved that Aesop was right. What is the unique strength of your business? The destiny of your business is to specialize by offering this unique strength to others.

Examples and Issues.

Child prodigies have an amazing strength.

Successful people specialize in their strength, sometimes starting as a young child. For example, Karl Benz graduated in mechanical engineering at nineteen, designed the first automobile, and co-founded Mercedes-Benz. You most likely know about these child prodigies: Wolfgang Amadeus Mozart (music), Shirley Temple (theatre), Tiger Woods (golf), and Bobby Fisher (chess).

I taught a child prodigy named Kenny. His mom carried him in for a Suzuki violin lesson and stood him up. With misgivings, I measured him for a tiny violin. During his lessons, I would chase him around the room on my knees. Kenny learned faster than the other children and led them during our group lessons. Impatiently he learned to play several songs on his violin. Kenny and his family moved away soon after he turned three. His next violin teacher didn't know what to do with Kenny.

Recently, I was sitting in the Daytona State College Orchestra next to Juaquin Trumpet. He started teaching himself to play the violin when he was twelve and continued for seven years. Our conductor, Norton Christiansen, announced Juaquin was judged the best string player enrolled in a state college in Florida.[4] He confided to me that he wanted to write sound tracks for movies. After our rehearsal, Juaquin delighted us with a spontaneous rendition of Henryk Wieniawski's Scherzo-Tarantelle, Op 16.

Should we treat others equally?

I believe we should not treat people equally because people do not want the same things. A blessing to one person is a curse to another. For example, a baby is a blessing to a loving couple, but a curse to a victim of incest. I believe that we're all blessed with a unique capability and we're driven to fulfill our destiny in our own way.

Should you improve your strengths or your weaknesses?

Schoolteachers want their students to improve their weaknesses. For example, they require weak readers to practice reading, weak writers to practice writing, and weak spellers to practice spelling.

I believe people should improve their weaknesses in school, but not in business. A business succeeds by specializing and improving its strengths. As Aesop advised, "You go further by using your own gift."

A generalist earns minimum wage.

One morning I taught my marketing students that a business profits by specializing in its strength. Then I rushed home to supervise an old man who was installing tiles on my porch. He groaned as he carried them and wore kneepads for kneeling on the hard tiles.

I wondered why he was still earning minimum wage at his age. He answered my unspoken question when he asked, "Do you want me to install cabinets, add crown molding, or paint walls? I can do anything."

This meant he could do nothing well enough to earn more money. With concern, I inspected the quality of his work. Sure enough, the tiles were not level. His work was not worth more than minimum wage.

Key #2: Compete on Strength.

What is the unique strength of your business?

Lots of businesses offer similar products and services, use similar technologies, and target similar customers, but what makes your business unique? Don't try to fit the mold, match the ratios, or duplicate "best practices." Your business will succeed by being as unique as a snowflake.

Ask your key customers, distributors, and suppliers this question: "Why are competitors envious of my business?" Some responses will not resonate with you, but when a response does resonate, you have identified the unique strength of your business. Specialize in this strength—it's your competitive advantage. Decide to compete on the unique strength of your business.

"You can't be all things to all people [...] Strategy is about making choices, trade-offs; it's about deliberately choosing to be different."
Michael [Eugene] Porter, Bishop William Lawrence University Professor at the Institute for Strategy and Competitiveness, Harvard Business School.

 Apply Key #2: Specialize in the Unique Strength of Your Business.

Generally speaking, how does your business compete?

- High quality

- Low prices

- Relationships with customers

If your business competes on high quality, how does your business achieve its high quality?

- Design and innovation

- Quality materials and/or services

- Reputation

- Other

If your business competes on low pricing, how does your business achieve its low prices?

- Efficiency

- Less overhead

- Low cost suppliers

- Other

If your business competes on relationships with customers, how does your business achieve this?

- Brand identity

- Custom products and/or services

- Empathy with customers

- Other

What specifically is the unique strength of your business?

"By virtue of exchange, one man's prosperity is beneficial to all others."
[Claude] Frederic Bastiat, advocate for free trade
and French libertarian, 1801–1850.

CHAPTER 3

Suppliers: How to Avoid Weaknesses

Be Lazy Like a Surfer Dude.

[Anthony] Tony Robbins, a peak performance coach, interviewed a surfer dude from California about his path to prosperity.[5] Frank Kern and his young family had been living in the back of a trailer. Frank said, "I had failed at selling door to door and everything else I tried."

Discouraged, Frank listened to a recording by Tony Robbins and implemented his coaching. Frank noticed a successful book about teaching a parrot to talk and was curious about why the book was so successful.

He used the Google Keyword Tool and Traffic Estimator to count the number of relevant Internet searches. Frank discovered that many people wanted to teach their parrot to talk.

"Being lazy, I realized that downloading an e-book is cheaper and easier than buying a book." Frank decided to fulfill their Internet searches with an e-book entitled *Teach Your Parrot to Talk*.

"I knew what information they wanted, but knew nothing about parrots or writing a book." Instead of being deterred, Frank delegated his weaknesses to a supplier. He borrowed $650 to pay a parrot expert to provide the information people sought on the Internet.

Frank specialized in his strength, Internet marketing, and advertised the e-book through Google Adwords. "I tried different ads to see which ad drove the most business." Soon his Adwords campaign was generating an income stream of three thousand dollars per month.

"I didn't know parrots, but I knew dogs." He created a course that taught dog owners how to use positive reinforcement with their dogs. As before, Frank advertised through Google Adwords and refined his campaign to generate more income.

"More people own dogs than parrots." Recognizing an opportunity, Frank revised the course for various breeds of dogs and designed six hundred different websites. "I pushed the button to launch all the websites at once." To his amazement, his courses generated $23.8 million within 24 hours.

Thrilled by his success, the new multimillionaire decided to teach others how to prosper from Internet marketing. His company, Instant Internet Empires, offered a collection of web templates for $47.77 and promised that "buyers could make more than $115,000 a year using the product."

You may remember a fuss about this promise because some buyers believed they could make money without using Frank's product. The result was that the Federal Trade Commission (FTC) issued a $247,000 judgment against Frank Kern and his company.[6]

The key to prosperity is not buying products, but using them. Like Frank Kern, your business can focus on quality, compete on strength, and delegate weaknesses. When you use *Aesop's Keys to Profitable Marketing* in your business, your business can spark its profits.

Can a Mouse Save a Lion?
An Aesop Tale

A mouse scampers over a lion's face. Awaking with a start, the lion seizes the mouse for a tasty meal. The mouse begs, "Please let me go and one day I'll repay your kindness." The lion chuckles and reluctantly lets him go.

Later, the lion is captured in a hunter's net. Responding to his desperate howls, the mouse runs over, gnaws through the net, and sets the lion free.

The mouse asserts, "You laughed at me, but even a lowly creature like a mouse can save the king of the animals."

Aesop advocates trading strengths with others because "a change of fortune can make the strongest man need a weaker man's help." Aesop advises a person to be "as good as his word."

Even the Strongest Need Help.

Is your business too poor to use suppliers?

Actually, the reverse is true. Your business is poor because it needs to use more suppliers. Let's see why this is true.

Suppliers are outside sources that can compensate for the weaknesses of your business and provide the expertise your business lacks. Even the largest business cannot excel at everything.

For example, business owners and managers hire contractors, landscapers, and repairmen to build and maintain their assets. Many hire consultants, advertising agencies, printers, and video producers to promote their business. Business owners and managers use distributors, sales representatives, shippers, warehouses, wholesalers, and retailers to facilitate transactions. They hire headhunters, insurance agents, lawyers, and trainers to deal with other weaknesses.

A business that delegates weaknesses can specialize in its strength. This means that the more your business delegates its weaknesses, the more it can specialize in its strength.

Should Your Business Use Suppliers?

How do strengths and weaknesses compare?

Let's see how much your business gains by using suppliers to compensate for its weaknesses. The 80/20 rule predicts the top 20% of the tasks will produce a 4-fold result (80%/20% = 4), whereas the bottom 80% of the tasks will only produce a meager result (20%/80% = .25).

Comparing top and bottom tasks (4/.25 = 16), we discover strengths produce 16 times more results than weaknesses. A wise entrepreneur delegates the bottom 80% of the tasks to suppliers, so the business can specialize in its strengths *(Figure 4)*.

Figure 4: Profits from Delegating

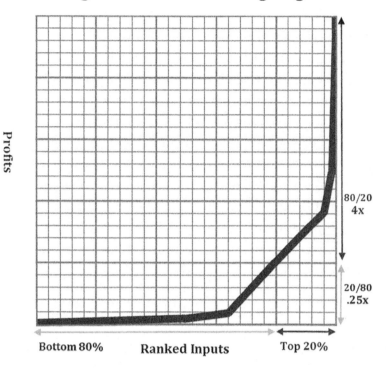

When a business trades its strengths to compensate for its weaknesses, both parties in the transaction become sixteen times more productive. For example, one of my weaknesses is filing taxes, whereas one my greatest strengths is coaching businesses. Holland Financial filed my taxes for me and I coached businesses on the company's radio show, *Real Money with David Holland*. Both parties greatly benefited from trading on our strengths. Specialize where your business is best and delegate the rest.

Should We Trade with Others?

What is the theory of comparative advantage?

Many think the United States should be self-sufficient and should block imports from other countries. Others think that trade increases prosperity, whether the trade is between two people, two businesses, or two countries. What do you think?

The theory of comparative advantage encourages you to specialize in items that you can produce more efficiently than others and to trade with suppliers for the other items. The theory states that you will benefit by producing and selling items in which you have a comparative advantage and by purchasing items in which you have a comparative disadvantage. Let's work out a simple example of the theory of comparative advantage.

A Thai worker can produce two iron rods or one cord of wood per hour, while a Korean worker can produce two iron rods or four cords of wood per hour *(Table 2)*.

Table 2: An Example of the Theory of Comparative Advantage

	Without Trade		With Specializing		With Trade	
	Thai	Korean	Thai	Korean	Thai	Korean
Iron	2	2	4		3	1
Wood	1	4		8	2	6

Since the Thai worker has a comparative advantage in producing iron rods, he benefits by only producing iron rods and trading them for cords of wood. In contrast, the Korean worker has a comparative advantage in producing cords of wood so he benefits by only producing cords of wood and trading them for iron rods. In two hours, the Thai worker can produce four iron rods, while the Korean worker can produce eight cords of wood.

Let's say the Thai worker trades one iron rod with the Korean worker for two cords of wood. Then the Thai worker ends up with three iron rods and two cords of wood, whereas the Korean worker ends up with one iron rod and six cords of wood.

Where did the extra three cords of wood come from? Trading increases the prosperity of both parties. Aesop says, "The strongest man needs a weaker man's help."

Does trade increase prosperity?

The theory of comparative advantage predicts that trade has a positive impact on prosperity. I tested whether this was true by analyzing eight years of economic data for eighty-seven countries. I assumed that a country exports its strengths (comparative advantages) and imports its weaknesses (comparative disadvantages).

The results consistently showed that exports, imports, and national prosperity had simultaneous, substantial, and synergistic relationships. Evidently, international trade significantly improved the prosperity of virtually all countries.

These results confirmed the theory of comparative advantage and verified that international trade has a positive impact on prosperity.[7] Clearly, countries prosper from low-cost imports and revenue-generating exports. Your business can also prosper by trading its strengths (comparative advantages) and delegating its weaknesses (comparative disadvantages).

How did trade improve the prosperity of Costa Rico?

When I first flew into Costa Rico, I saw a patchwork of pineapple plantations. Their owners were basking in prosperity like regal lions. The country's climate and soil were ideal for growing pineapples. But without warning, a parasite devastated their crops and crushed the economy of Costa Rica.

The World Bank loaned money to Costa Rica to solve its economic crisis. Consultants discovered that Costa Rica was ideal for growing African coconut palms. They predicted its citizens would be able to assemble computer chips, while its natural beauty, culture, and safety would attract tourists. The government taught plantation owners to plant African coconut palms and loaned money to developers for building computer chip factories and facilities for tourists.

On my next flight into Costa Rica, I saw orderly plantations of African coconut palms, industrial parks, and coastal resorts. The plantations exported coconut oil for lotions and the factories exported computer chips. The government's website, Anywhere Costa Rica, attracted tourists to its resorts, parks, beaches, and zip line canopy tours. New roads connected prosperous villages to urban centers. Costa Rica had become the most prosperous country in Central America.

Key #3: Delegate Weaknesses.

Should you trade skills like a lazy lion?

Yes, you will prosper by trading your strengths for your weaknesses. Be lazy and contract with suppliers that can compensate for your weaknesses. Your business can only specialize in its strengths if it delegates its weaknesses.

If your business specializes in the top twenty percent of its tasks, its suppliers will be sixteen times better at its remaining tasks than your business. Others love to do what you hate. The path to prosperity is not self-sufficiency, but interdependency. Decide to delegate the weaknesses of your business to suppliers.

"The essence of strategy is choosing what not to do."
Michael [Eugene] Porter, Bishop William Lawrence University Professor at the Institute for Strategy and Competitiveness, Harvard Business School, an authority on economic development.

 Apply Key #3: Delegate the Weaknesses of Your Business to Suppliers.

What are weaknesses of your business?

- Accounting
- Collections
- Customer service
- Customer training
- Direct sales
- Employee training
- Engineering
- Finance
- Fulfillment

- Global business
- Innovation
- Insurance
- Legal issues
- Management
- Market research
- Personnel
- Planning
- Production

- Promotion
- Repairs
- Retailing
- Returns
- Shipping

- Sourcing
- Storage
- Technology
- Wholesaling

What specific functions, tasks, and projects will your business delegate to relevant suppliers?

CHAPTER 4

Target Market: How to Describe Key Customers

Harley-Davidson Restores a Legend.

Prior to and during the world wars, Harley-Davidson prospered from its legendary reputation. In 1969, the American Machine and Foundry (AMF) bought the company. AMF decided to compete for customers with cheap Japanese motorcycles. In its greed for more customers, AMF reduced Harley's quality, tarnished its reputation, and slid toward bankruptcy.

Twelve years later, Willie G. Davidson and his friends saved Harley-Davidson from bankruptcy. Its new owners noticed that Harley's most profitable customers kept buying its products.

Harley delighted these key customers with "retro" American styling, branded accessories, and events sponsored by Harley Owner Groups (HOG). As a result, Harley restored its legendary reputation, attracted highly profitable new customers, and regained its profitability.

Is Haste a Waste?
An Aesop Tale

A Greek god rewards a worshiper with a goose. The man grumbles to his wife, "Why did Hermes give us a goose?" The next morning he discovers why—the goose laid a golden egg! Awaking the next day with great anticipation, the man finds another golden egg.

Day after day after day he finds another golden egg and another and another. Eventually, his gratitude sours into a feeling of entitlement. "Why must I wait for wealth to come in driblets? The inside of the goose must be solid gold!"

Hastily, he slaughters the goose and opens up its belly. To his horror, all he finds is blood and guts like any ordinary bird. Bewailing his fate, he sobs, "Woe is me. I've killed the goose that laid golden eggs."

Aesop advises that haste is a waste. "In their hunger for wealth, greedy people destroy what they already value." The "greedy lose all" because they "have much, yet want more."

Key Customers Lay Golden Eggs.

Your business is blessed with a wealth-producing asset—its loyal, heavy users. Cherish your most profitable customers and they will keep "laying golden eggs" year after year. A business that delights its key customers can easily attract highly profitable new customers.

However, greedy entrepreneurs "have much, yet want more." In their hunger for more customers, they neglect their most profitable customers. Greedy entrepreneurs assume "our most profitable customers will always buy from us," but customer loyalty is soured by neglect.

How Valuable Are Your Key Customers?

Should you treat customers equally?

No, some customers are much more valuable to your business than others since your business is more valuable to them. Delight your key customers and you will be delighted with your profits.

You realize the top 20% of your customers will produce 80% of your profits, but the Pareto distribution predicts some customers are even more valuable.

- The top 4% ($20\%^2$) of your customers will produce 64% of your profits ($80\%^2$).

- The top .8% ($20\%^3$) of your customers will produce 51% of your profits ($80\%^3$).

- The top .16% ($20\%^4$) of your customers will produce 41% of your profits ($80\%^4$) (*Figure 5*).

Figure 5: Profits from Key Customers

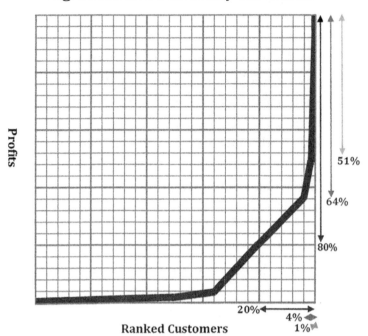

Focus on your best customers since they are willing to buy a ridiculous amount from your business. Once you identify them, offer them your premium package and never let them go. Treat these customers like they are laying golden ostrich eggs.

Are your best customers really this profitable?

Many scientists have shown these predictions are actually true. For example, Pareto confirmed more than a hundred years ago that the Pareto distribution is a universal law of nature. Whenever he plotted a large unbiased sample of data on standard graph paper, he saw the Pareto distribution, but whenever he plotted the same data on log-log graph paper, he saw a straight line *(Figure 6)*.

Figure 6: The Pareto Distribution on a Log-Log Plot

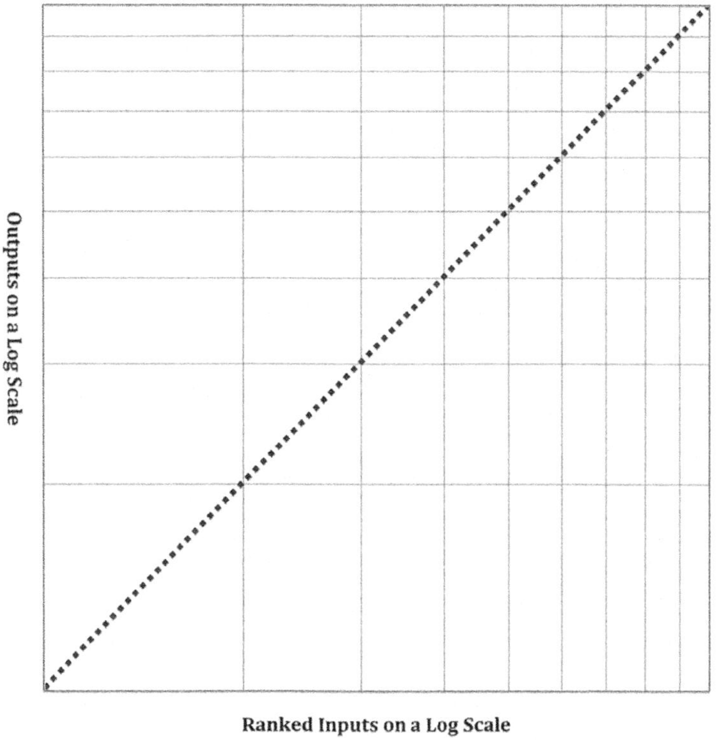

Outputs on a Log Scale

Ranked Inputs on a Log Scale

In January 2005, Mark E. J. Newman, a brilliant physicist at Bell Laboratories, plotted the repetitions in a large sample of random numbers. The data points traced a Pareto distribution on standard graph paper and a straight line on log-log graph paper.[8] Newman's research verifies the Pareto distribution is a universal law of nature.

Was I a Goose?

A company hired me to sell marketing research projects and agreed to pay me a hefty salary plus a ten percent sales commission. During my first week on the job, I called my prior client at Caremark Pharmacy Services (Caremark) to see if the subsidiary of CVS Caremark Corporation needed marketing research.

Instead of marketing research, Caremark needed employee research. Caremark manages prescription benefits for large employers and Caremark planned to evaluate employee satisfaction with its services. Since Caremark admired my previous work, its board of directors wanted to meet me and my new employer.

In the meeting, the owner presented the capabilities of his marketing research company. "We have conducted customer satisfaction studies for many years."

I stood up and explained, "Our experience prepares us to measure employee satisfaction with Caremark's management of prescription benefits."

The owner continued, "Most of our clients are banks."

"Since I have conducted several marketing research projects for Caremark, I understand your business and how you benefit your clients. I can easily conduct employee satisfaction studies for you."

The owner concluded, "Our customer satisfaction studies typically show that ninety-eight percent of the customers are delighted with our clients' services."

"Based upon our experience, Caremark can expect its clients' employees to be delighted with your management of their prescription benefits."

After the presentation, the project manager expressed his delight with my responses and asked me how long I had worked for the owner. "Only two weeks."

The project manager whispered in my ear, "The owner better watch out. In another year, you'll be the owner."

Caremark contracted with the owner for annual employee evaluations of its services for each of their clients. His marketing research company would greatly profit from these repetitious studies and Caremark would become one of its key customers.

Within a few weeks, I had sold some other highly profitable research projects. But instead of paying me $78,000 in sales commissions, the owner of the marketing research company abruptly fired me. When my clients learned this, his company lost the projects. Did the owner realize that he "killed a goose that laid golden eggs?"

Key #4: Describe Key Customers.

How do you describe key customers?

The first step is to select an unbiased sample of a hundred customers of your business. Your sample will represent the diversity of your customers if you set quotas on relevant demographics.

Let's say that half of your customers are men, less than forty years old, and live in Daytona Beach, Florida. Then your quotas would be half men and half women, half under forty and half at least forty, and half living in Daytona Beach and half living elsewhere.

The next step is to evaluate the profitability of each customer in your sample. Profitability can be defined as the profit per item times the number of items purchased during a certain time period. The most profitable twenty customers in your sample will represent the most profitable twenty percent of your customers.

Interview these key customers in depth so you understand their purchase motivations and buying processes. Describe how they differ from your other customers and profile their typical traits.

For example, the key customers of Harley-Davidson tend to be mature American white men with a technical profession who identify with the Harley lifestyle and glory in their conservative values. They usually socialize with other Harley enthusiasts, customize their bikes, and borrow money to upgrade them.

The profile is quite different for key customers of Holland Financial Services (HFS) in Ormond Beach, Florida. They are usually wealthy mature women who are highly educated, open-minded and achievement-oriented and who invest with HFS after a major change in their life.

Joseph La Bosco's Jewelry & Pawn, Daytona Beach, Florida, has two sets of customers: people who pawn items and people who buy the items. Key customers who pawn items tend to be people on social security or disability benefits who have a financial emergency. In contrast, key customers who buy items tend to be foreign bargain hunters on eBay.

Once you have profiled the key customers of your business, decide to target them with your marketing decisions.

"The aim of marketing is to know and understand the customers
so well the product or service fits him and sells itself."
Peter F. Drucker, developer of management by objectives,
management consultant and author, 1909–2005.

Apply Key #4: Describe and Target Your Key Customers.

Profile the typical traits of your key customers and their household on relevant demographic variables:

- Head of household
    - ○ Education
    - ○ Language
    - ○ Race
- Employment
    - ○ Income
    - ○ Industry
    - ○ Status
- Location
    - ○ Description
    - ○ Geography
    - ○ Longevity
- Residents
    - ○ Age
    - ○ Gender
    - ○ Marriage

Profile the typical traits of your key customers on relevant aspects of their lifestyle:

- Activities
    - ○ Habits
    - ○ Hobbies
    - ○ Events
- Beliefs
    - ○ Attitudes
    - ○ Values
    - ○ Opinions
- Media
    - ○ Usage
    - ○ Purchases
    - ○ Influences
- Passages
    - ○ Life stage
    - ○ Aspirations
    - ○ Issues

Profile the typical traits of your key customers on relevant aspects of their buying behavior:

- Motivation
  - ○ Catalyst
  - ○ Timing
  - ○ Frequency

- Priorities
  - ○ Features
  - ○ Benefits
  - ○ Value

- Search process
  - ○ Length
  - ○ Influences
  - ○ Complexity

What are the typical traits of your key customers on relevant aspects of their demographics, lifestyle, and buying behavior?

CHAPTER 5

Products and Services: How to Offer Benefits

The Product That Wasn't.

In 1983, Dr. Kenneth Bernhardt taught a class about product development at Georgia State University in Atlanta, Georgia. For my term project, I met with the vice president of marketing at the Kimberly-Clark Corporation. The company manufactured a plastic "felt-like" fabric that was both waterproof and air permeable. Since the fabric was coarse and difficult to dye, Kimberly-Clark did not know what to do with its invention.

Being empathetic with athletes, I realized this waterproof, yet breathable fabric was ideal for sports applications. At a low cost, Kimberly-Clark could manufacture sleeping bags, tents, and sports apparel out of the seamless fabric. Athletes would prefer this fabric to Gore-Tex because water would not leak through seams.

Several years later I overheard someone ask a Gore-Tex executive if the company had any competitors. "Not really. Kimberly-Clark had the capability, but they never realized they could have blown us out of the water."

When Is a Fox Hungry?
An Aesop Tale

A fox invites his friend to dinner and serves her a delicious soup in a flat dish. The fox slurps up the soup and licks his lips with great relish. He snickers at the stork's efforts to suck up the soup with her bill and she flies away.

Later, the stork plays a similar prank on the fox. She invites the fox to dinner and serves him a delicious soup in a tall pitcher. The stork eagerly sucks up the soup with her bill and giggles at his efforts to reach the broth with his tongue. The fox goes home hungry with his tail between his legs.

Aesop's fable encourages us to be empathetic with others and offer "different strokes for different folks."

Offer Treasures to Key Customers.

Different strokes for different folks.

Aesop's tale teaches us to be empathic. For example, serve soup to a fox in a flat dish, but serve soup to a stork in a pitcher. If you compromise with a cup, both the fox and stork will go hungry. If you try to please all customers, you will end up pleasing no one.

Provide products and services your most profitable customers will treasure. They are sixteen times more profitable than your other customers and would pay higher prices to get exactly what they want.

However, your other customers are price sensitive so they seek inexpensive commodities. These brand switchers provide only twenty percent of your profits so discontinue any products and services that do not delight your key customers.

Prune products and services.

I loved to prune the lilacs around my house. One year I pruned so much my neighbors said I had killed the lilacs. But soon their branches sprouted and bloomed more than ever before. Pruning strengthens lilacs—and a business. Like lilacs, your business must prune unprofitable products and services. The savings can be used to add value to more profitable items.

Brand managers often fight to protect their brands as if their careers depended upon it. They reinvent brands, launching "new improved versions" even though the brands deserve a respectful funeral.

Only offer items your key customers will treasure. Your business will profit from offering fewer products and services since more options confuse customers, whereas fewer options increase sales.[9] For example, car manufacturers confuse their customers by offering too many choices. In contrast, Henry Ford offered the Model T Ford in "any color so long as it is black."[10]

Which Items Are Not Very Profitable?

How much should your business prune items?

As predicted by the Pareto distribution, most of your products and services are not very profitable.

- Pruning 80 of 100 items loses 20% (100% – 80% = 20%) of profits.

- Pruning 96 ($20\%^2$ = 4%) of 100 items loses 36% (100% – $80\%^2$ = 36%) of profits.

- Pruning 99 ($20\%^3$ = .8%) of 100 items loses 49% (100% – $80\%^3$ = 49%) of profits.

Conversely, one item produces 51% of the profits. Wise entrepreneurs keep their treasures, discontinue other products and services, and launch new items their key customers will treasure *(Figure 7)*.

Figure 7: Prune Products and Services

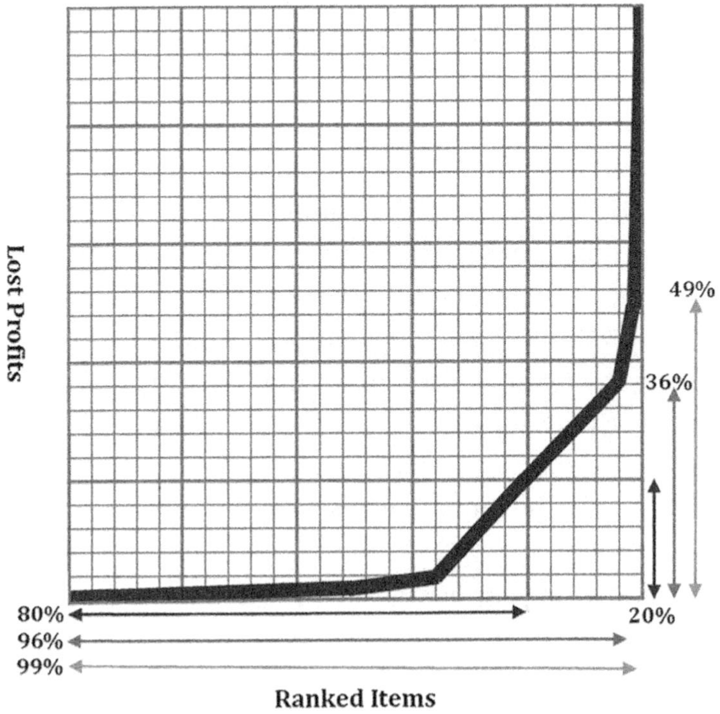

Ranked Items

Ways to Offer Treasures.

Simplify features.

In the 1950s, IBM began using the 80/20 rule to simplify its software. Research showed that its customers used twenty percent of the functions eighty percent of the time. In response, IBM put popular functions on drop down menus and relegated unpopular functions to less conspicuous locations. Later other software developers and manufacturers did the same.

Prune options.

Pillsbury appointed Herman Cain as President and CEO of Godfather's Pizza. Upon his arrival in 1986, Cain told employees, "We are not dead. Our objective is to prove to Pillsbury and everyone else that we will survive."[11]

Soon afterward Cain visited a restaurant and looked at the confusing array of pizza toppings. "Which toppings are not requested much." Cain eliminated these topping from all restaurants in the franchise. Cain credits a single overriding principle for his success—"focus, focus, focus."[12]

Innovate for key customers.

Bluebeam Software, Inc. (Bluebeam) leverages the PDF format into smart, simple solutions for a paperless workflow. Its customers are architecture, engineering, and construction (AEC) firms, as well as government agencies, manufacturers, detailers, and drafters. Richard Lee, Bluebeam's President and CEO:

> We're relentlessly working to mimic the way you normally work with pen and paper [...] Our customers need to keep projects moving whether they are in an

office, at the job site or on a camping trip, and the technology in Revu 12 makes it easier to finish projects faster and work better.[13]

The software simplifies PDF creation, markup, editing, and collaboration technology. Joe Giaudrone, Assistant Project Manager at Schuchart Corporation, testifies about Bluebeam:

> It does about 300% more than the Adobe product. Not to sound like a huge nerd or anything, but every time one of us finds a new helpful feature we get excited and giddy to show it off to one another and to rub it in our colleagues' faces who are still using the Adobe product.[14]

Discontinue unprofitable products.

Sea-Doo, the personal watercraft (PWC) brand of Bombardier Recreational Products, developed product lines that appeal to market segments of its customers.

- The Tow Sport line appeals to families who cannot afford a standard boat. Members of this market segment love to tow one another and seek a powerful engine, rear-view mirror, and re-boarding step.

- The Recreation line appeals to couples who explore waterways on one PWC. These couples seek a stable boat with a comfortable seat, reliable engine, and large gas tank.

- The Performance line appeals to young men who enjoy thrills and seek a maneuverable boat, high-performance engine, and a big plume.

- The Luxury line appeals to wealthy couples who host parties at their lake home and provide a fleet of upscale Sea-Doos for their guests.

The most profitable customers buy Luxury Sea-Doos while its less profitable customers buy other Sea-Doos. Since these lines dilute the reputation of the Luxury line, I believe Sea-Doo could increase its profits by discontinuing less profitable product lines and upgrading the value and reputation of its Luxury line.

Key #5: Offer Treasures.

Secrets of a successful startup.

For six years, I taught marketing and research courses at Bethune-Cookman University in Daytona Beach, Florida. Most of my students were blacks who were raised by a single mother and were the first in their family to attend college. The Business students expected successful people to occupy a corner office, carry a heavy briefcase, and wear a black suit.

I ran my Principle of Marketing classes like a business incubator. The marketing students wrote strategic marketing plans, implemented their plans, and kept the profits. Only four did not earn profits, and most students earned at least seven hundred dollars within two months.

I taught them *Keys to Profitable Marketing* such as how to focus on quality, compete on strength, delegate weaknesses, describe key customers, and offer treasures. They knew what their fellow students wanted, delighted them with their products and services, and took pride in running a successful startup.

My best student found a cheap supplier of laptops in China and sold them to her fellow students. She took orders before purchasing them through PayPal and easily earned thousands of dollars.

She inspired other students to be entrepreneurial. For example, a student on the girls' basketball team provided manicures while traveling to and from their games. Some provided computer support, cut hair, led exercise classes, or provided transportation.

One student manufactured and sold teeth grills to black men. His mother worried that he would never be successful, but I told her, "He's already making lots of money selling grills. He will use these skills in a corporate career."

Can you do likewise?

Although skilled at marketing to their friends, none of my marketing students crossed the bridge to the peninsula. They were not willing to market items to an unfamiliar market segment. Are you willing to "cross the bridge" and market to people who are different from you?

Exactly what products and services do your key customers want and why do they value them? Do they seek a goal, desire a lifestyle, or crave an identity like Harley bikers? Do they want to maintain a pleasant situation like tourists in Costa Rica? Do they want to escape from an unpleasant situation like engineers using Bluebeam software?

For example, why did you buy *Aesop's Keys to Profitable Marketing*?

- To increase your profits, obtain a prosperous lifestyle, or be an entrepreneur?

- To enjoy reading its stories and examples?

- To escape from an unpleasant boss, the burden of debt, or unemployment?

In your business, decide to add value to items that your key customers treasure and to discontinue other products and services.

"If advertisers spent the same amount of money on improving products as they do on advertising them, they wouldn't have to advertise them."
Will [Penn Adair] Rogers, cowboy, vaudeville performer,
actor, humorist, author, and columnist, 1879–1935.

 ### Apply Key #5: Offer Treasures to Your Key Customers.

Describe the ideal product or service for your key customers on these traits.

- Features
- Styling
- Quality
- Packaging

- Reputation and endorsements
- Risk reduction
- Customer support
- Aftermarket parts

Which products and services do your key customers treasure?

How will your business improve the value of products or services for your key customers?

Which items will be discontinued?

"We get real results only in proportion to the real values we give."
James Cash Penney, entrepreneur,
founder of J. C. Penney Company, Inc., 1875–1971.

CHAPTER 6

Pricing: How to Set Prices

Convert Junk into Treasures.

For decades Gaye and Frank, have run a successful eBay business named "Soup to Nuts." They prove one person's junk is another person's treasure by selling junk for high prices. The couple prowls garage sales, estate auctions, and flea markets for junk their customers will treasure.

Their most profitable customers are collectors. You name it, they collect it: etched glass, baseball cards, costume jewelry, shoes for diabetics, iconic purses, and on and on. Their home abounds with treasures.

Gaye and Frank respond with empathy for their "Internet friends." My cousins recognize items in the junk that specific customers will treasure. These key customers will gladly pay high prices to enhance their collections and my cousins are richly rewarded for transforming junk into treasures.

What Saves an Apple Tree?
An Aesop Tale

A peasant decides to cut down an apple tree that produces no fruit. Sparrows who roost in its branches beg him to spare the barren tree. "Our merry chirping enlivens your work in the garden. If you destroy our home, we must leave you to work alone."

Ignoring their pleas, the peasant raises his ax for the first blow. Before he strikes, he notices its trunk is hollow. Hidden inside is a beehive brimming over with delicious honey.

Overjoyed, the peasant drops his ax and exclaims, "The old tree is worth keeping after all."

Aesop reminds us that value is in the eye of the beholder. One person's junk is another person's treasure. "Utility is most men's test of worth."

Key Customers Will Pay the Price.

How much will your key customers pay?

The chirping of swallows is worthless to the peasant, but he values honey. The peasant keeps the old apple tree so its beehive will provide him an endless supply of delicious honey.

Your business can increase the worth of your products and services in three ways.

- Fulfill your customers' desire for a product, service, emotion, or self-concept like Harley-Davidson does.

- Maintain your customers in a pleasant situation like Costa Rica does.

- Relieve your customers' pain, lower their risk, ease their effort, and improve their emotion like Bluebeam software does.

Charging too little will discredit a product or service's value. Customers will perceive its materials are shoddy, its design is obsolete, and its reputation is tarnished. For example, pricing your home too low encourages prospective buyers to imagine all sorts of problems such as a leaky basement, high utility bills, and noisy neighbors.

If your key customers treasure your products and services, you can charge higher prices. Your customers will assume your items must be worth the price. In fact, my status-seeking cousin bragged that she bought her house for more than the asking price.

Learn from my success.

Finding the sweet spot for pricing is difficult, but not impossible. For example, I priced five of my own homes at 1 percent below their market value and obtained my asking price by adding value.

- The first couple avoided storage costs by storing their possessions in my home before the closing date.

- The second family could not obtain a loan so I financed their loan myself.

- The third family wanted to close before the end of the year so I expedited the transaction.

- The fourth family obtained our riding lawn mower.

The fifth house was on such a steep hill that my next door neighbor used a pulley system to mow his lawn. I turned this problem into an asset by advertising its "commanding view of a forest." I waited as a prospective buyer gazed over the forest and once again I obtained my asking price.

Learn from my mistake.

I developed and sold perceptual mapping software for $495 in 42 countries. MapWise was the first commercial software for correspondence analysis in English.

Then I promoted a new version of MapWise for $9.95 to all members of the American Marketing Association. To my dismay, only three recipients responded to the direct mail promotion.

Did the low price imply that MapWise was difficult, inaccurate, and infected with bugs? Actually, the $9.95 version was better than the $495 version. The new version was easier, more accurate, and better tested than the old version.

Later a highly respected company bundled correspondence analysis with other perceptual mapping software and charged a steep price for the package. When I tested the company's correspondence analysis module, the software was difficult, inaccurate, and froze up. Its buyers must have assumed from its high price that the software had a high quality.

How Much Can Your Business Profit from Higher Prices?

The 80/20 rule predicts that 80 percent of your customers only account for 20 percent of your profits. These customers are sensitive about price and may switch to a lower-priced competitor if you increase your price.

The other 20 percent of your customers are less sensitive about price and account for 80 percent of your profits. They will remain loyal heavy users of your business if you gradually increase the price. If you don't raise your price, you are leaving money on the table.

This example shows how much your profits can grow when your business improves its pricing strategy in three steps.

Step One.

Your business cannot make much profit using the commodity pricing strategy. For example, if the cost per item is $100 and the competition charges $100 for a similar item, your business cannot compete on price. If your price were $100, then your total cost would equal your total revenue (*Table 3*).

Table 3: Steps in Pricing as Valued

Pricing Strategy	Price	Cost	Customers	Total Cost	Total Revenue	Total Profit
Commodity Pricing	$100	$100	100	$10,000	$10,000	$0
Value-Added Pricing	$200	$150	20	$3,000	$4,000	$1,000
Price Skimming	$200	$150	100	$15,000	$20,000	$5,000

Step Two.

Your business can increase its profit per item using the value-added pricing strategy. For example, if your business spends $50 more per item and its key customers perceive the item is now worth $100 more than its competition, your business can double the price to $200. However, 80 customers will switch to a competitor. If 20 customers buy at the higher price, the total cost is $3,000, revenue is $4,000 and profit is $1,000.

Step Three.

Your business can multiply its profits using the price skimming strategy. For example, your business can target prospects who are similar to your key customers and convert them into highly profitable new customers. These key prospects can replace the eighty customers the business lost when it raised its price. If a hundred customers pay $200 for the item, then the total cost is $15,000, revenue is $20,000, and profit is $5,000.

Pricing Mistakes.

Sea-Doo's product line.

Sea-Doo publicized the starting prices for its lines of Personal Watercraft (PWC) as follows: Rec Lite line at $4,999, Recreation at $8,199, Tow Sport at $11,699, Performance at $11,899, and Luxury at $12,199.

The production costs for each PWC are probably similar so Sea-Doo must be losing money on its Rec Lite line and earning the highest profits on its Luxury line. Based upon my research, buyers of the Luxury line are social climbers who would brag, "Our friends deserve the best, so we bought the best PWCs to entertain our guests."

I believe Sea-Doo should discontinue its less prestigious lines and increase the perceived value of its Luxury line. Then Sea-Doo could increase its overall profits by hiking the price of its Luxury line.

No hassle, no haggle pricing.

Like most women, I hate to haggle over prices at an automobile dealership. "I'm afraid I might end up paying more than a man." A male friend haggled over the price of his new car and obtained such a low price that I insisted on the same deal.

Yes, I did obtain the same price, but the salesman detested my doggedness. I watched him order a technician to drill holes in my new car for an expensive luggage rack. "If I had not bought the ugly rack, water would have leaked into my trunk."

Several years later my employer asked me to check out Saturn's "no haggle, no hassle pricing" policy as claimed by its advertising:

> The worst part of the car-buying experience is the car-buying experience. There's a better way, the Saturn way. Savor the great price and our no haggle, no hassle policy. Experience the Saturn difference.[15]

True to its word, the Saturn dealership did not haggle over prices nor hassle me. Basking in their respect for me, I impulsively traded my car for a Saturn.

Key #6: Price as Valued.

How much do key customers value your products and services?

Setting prices is a difficult marketing decision, but marketing research can reveal the price sensitivity of your key customers.

For example, my marketing research class at the Thunderbird School of Global Management in Glendale, Arizona, helped a Swedish company, Malaco, price its candy. Swedish Fish are pastel-colored, fish-shaped gummi candy with a licorice flavor. My class and I hated the candy, but its key customers were children.

The closest competitor to Swedish Fish was Gummi Bears. My students asked children to taste the two types of candy and trade them. "How many Gummi Bears do you trade for ten Swedish Fish?" Trading identified the value of Swedish Fish relative to its closest competitor. As a result, the company introduced Swedish Fish at the right price for the United States market.

Only your key customers know how much they value your products and services. Decide to price items by their value to your key customers.

> *"Pricing is actually a pretty simple and straightforward thing. Customers will not pay literally a penny more than the true value of the product."*
> Ron Johnson, a retailing expert for Target and Apple.

 Apply Key #6: Price as Valued by Your Key Customers.

What most directly competes with your product or service and what is its price?

What does your product or service achieve for your key customers?

- Progress toward a desired outcome
  - More achievement
  - More confidence
  - Better relationship
  - Better reputation

- Maintenance of a pleasant situation
  - Personal attention
  - Joy
  - Lifestyle

- Escape from an unpleasant situation
  - Less effort
  - Less risk
  - Less pain
  - Less bad emotion

How much is this worth to them?

At what price would your key customers buy your competitor's offering instead of yours?

Set your price slightly lower than this amount.

How much will your key customers pay for the products and services they treasure?

"Have the courage to follow your heart and intuition."
Steven [Paul] Jobs, a father of the Digital Revolution, co-founder of Apple, Inc. and Pixar, founder of NeXT Inc., 1955–2011.

CHAPTER 7

Distribution: How to Build Loyalty

Out with the Old, In with the New.

Distribution channels use different marketing strategies than the products and services they distribute. For example, Seaman's Furniture was a chain of traditional furniture stores. Its customers complained about its limited assortment, high prices, and slow delivery. Before long, the business was on the brink of bankruptcy.

Jeffrey Seaman and his son Morty paid off their debt by starting a chain of innovative furniture stores. Rooms To Go consistently delighted its key customers with a broad assortment, low prices, and fast delivery. Currently, Rooms To Go Incorporated employs more than seven thousand employees and generates billions in sales each year.

Why Did a Tortoise Beat a Hare?
An Aesop Tale

A tortoise and a hare argue about who is swifter. They decide to settle the dispute with a race. The hare has such confidence in his natural fleetness that he does not worry about the race and brags, "The tortoise is so slow I can snooze by the wayside and still win the race." He lies down and falls asleep.

The tortoise is acutely conscious of his slow movements. Unfazed by the cocky hare, the tortoise plods along affirming, "I never stop, I never stop, I never ever stop."

Eventually, the tortoise passes the hare as he snoozes. When the hare wakes up, he desperately chases the tortoise. Unable to catch up for lost time, the hare watches in horror as the tortoise crosses the finish line first. The tortoise wins the race!

Aesop observes, "A naturally gifted man, through lack of application, is often beaten by a plodder." Consistency wins the prize and winners are "slow but sure."

Consistently Delight Your Key Customers.

What wins customer loyalty?

Although the tortoise was slower than the hare, he won the race because his consistency compensated for his slowness. Distribution channels win the prize of customer loyalty by consistently delighting their key customers.

Are customers delighted in the same way?

My friends and I were enjoying a highbrow art show in West Palm Beach, Florida. As I admired a painting by Chagall, a well-dressed stranger approached me and raved about my shirt. "How can I buy one just like it?" "I bought this shirt at Penney's." "I would never shop at Penney's! Where did you really buy your shirt?" "This shirt was a Christmas present for my mother-in-law, but she didn't like it. The shirt is on sale at Penney's for under fifteen dollars"

The next day my husband and I strolled down Worth Avenue in Palm Beach, Florida. After gawking at the expensive boutiques, I shyly entered one and tried on a coat with ravels drooping from its sleeves. Afterward I commented to my husband, "Who would pay $3,000 for raggedy coat like that?"

When we returned to the parking lot, I noticed the stranger and she proudly showed me her purchase. She asked me to model her new coat as she took pictures. I quickly stuffed its ravels inside its sleeves.

When she was out of earshot, my husband and I laughed at her crazy attitude toward retailers. "She buys raggedy clothes at boutiques, but I buy stylish clothes at Penney's."

How can your business delight its key customers?

In 2012, Wal-Mart Stores, Inc. earned $467,896,000 in revenues worldwide, more than the Gross National Product (GNP) of most countries.[16] The chain delights its key customers by consistently delivering their three favorite benefits: convenience, assortment, and cost-efficiency.

- Almost all U.S. households are conveniently located within 60 miles of a Wal-Mart store.

- Most Wal-Mart stores include an assortment of specialty shops such as a restaurant, bank, an optical shop, beauty shop, and nail salon.

- The cost efficiency of Wal-Mart Stores, Inc. resulted in estimated savings in 2007 of at least $287 billion, which equates to $957 per person or $2,500 per household.[17]

Successful distribution channels delight their key customers in various ways:

- Representatives of Mary Kay, Inc. prioritize personal service, training, and guarantees of its beauty products.

- Owners of Hallmark Gold Crown stores prioritize social status, enjoyment, and packaging.

- The employees of GoDaddy.com, LLC, prioritize speed, technical support, and reminders.

- Sales clerks at hhgregg, inc. prioritize point-of purchase promotions, product expertise, and financing.

Examples of Distribution Channels

Marjorie's Rugs.

Georgette wanted to celebrate her family's homecoming with the purchase of a unique runner for their entryway. On her way home from work, Georgette drove slowly down a major shopping street, checking out carpet stores in Port Orange, Florida.

Most signs bragged about their low prices, but Marjorie's Rugs offered high-quality rugs. She browsed through Marjorie's Rugs, each rug more gorgeous than the one before. "Marjorie showed me rugs that harmonized with our Chinese-American décor. She helped me find runners that are the right size and let me try them out at home."

Georgette heaped rolls of runners into her car and drove home. She displayed the rugs to her husband and daughter and they clapped with delight when she showed them her favorite rug. The next day, she returned the rugs to the store and bought her favorite one, barely noticing its high price.

Georgette proudly showed off the runner to her neighbors. All loved how the runner enhanced her décor. Marjorie's Rugs had earned a generous profit and attracted new customers as well.

Meet Dr. Don, a sales professional.

Dr. Don put himself through medical school by selling pots and pans. During his internship, he observed an operating room emergency. The patient died and her family sued another intern for medical malpractice. Dr. Don was so upset that he vowed to never practice medicine. Instead, he continued to sell pots and pans.

Dr. Don offered to show me how to succeed at sales. With skepticism, I shadowed him during his appointment with a Caribbean nurse and her husband. He rang the doorbell and leaned down to inspect a plant on the front porch. When the nurse came to the door, Dr. Don said, "This is such a lovely plant. You must be nurturing the plant with tender, loving care."

"Yes, I water it carefully and trim the blooms." "You must be Mrs. Smith. I'm honored to meet you." "Please come in Dr. Don." "Just call me Don. Where would you like me to sit?" "You can sit here at our kitchen table." "May I put my boxes of samples here?" "Of course. This is my husband." "Good afternoon, Mr. Smith. I'm pleased to meet you. Your home is so attractive and comfortable. You two must really enjoy your time at home." "Yes we do."

After building rapport with the couple, Don inquired, "Please excuse my question, but we need to know the answer. I apologize for prying, but at the end of the month, how much do you have left after you have paid for your home, your utilities, food, insurance, taxes, and other necessities?" After a discussion, they agreed they usually have twenty dollars left at the end of the month.

Looking around, Don gazed with admiration at a bookshelf. "Mr. Smith, did you build this handsome bookshelf?" "Oh yes, I built it for our home." "You must really love your wife to build her such a handsome bookshelf." "Yes I do." "Did you use high-quality tools?" "Yes, I have a full set of carpenter tools."

Don asked him, "Does your wife cook good meals for you?" "Oh, yes, I love her cooking." "Does your wife deserve high-quality tools?" "Yes, she does." Don turned to Mrs. Smith. "Do you love to cook for your husband?" "Indeed." "Would you please show us your pots and pans?"

She returned with dreadful pots and pans and Don inspected them with concern. After pondering how much they could afford, Don put a form on the table and asked Mrs. Smith for a pen. She quickly handed him a pen and the couple signed the form without any discussion.

"I'll bring your pots and pans to your home in a week. Do you have a friend who cooks great meals for her husband?" With great pride, they promised to refer him to their friends. Don picked up his samples and graciously bid them goodbye.

Afterward I realized that Don did not show them any pots or pans, tell them the monthly payment, nor disclose the length of the contract. Then I understood how my friend had become a millionaire.

Which Distribution Channels Are Best?

The best ones consistently delight your key customers. Retain the top twenty percent of your distribution channels, find similar ones, and prune the other ones *(Figure 8)*.

Figure 8: Deliver Delight

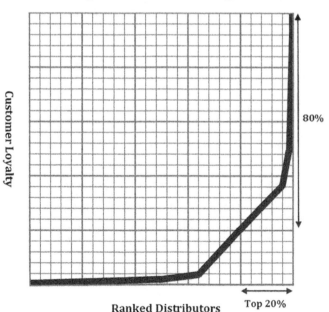

Customer Loyalty

80%

Ranked Distributors   Top 20%

Key #7: Deliver Delight.

I usually challenge my International Marketing students to guess the biggest export from the United States. My students usually mention obvious items like cars, weapons, or software. A student from Eastern Europe guessed, "Franchises." Astonished, I realized he was right! When I visited Japan more than forty years ago, we had a "Mac Attack" and headed for McDonald's. Today travelers see franchises from the United States in every major city around the world.

Until recently, the top ten franchises were headquartered in the United States. In descending order they are Subway, McDonald's, 7-Eleven, Hampton Inn & Suites, Great Clips, H&R Block, Dunkin' Donuts, Jani-King, Servpro, and MiniMarkets.[18] On September 1, 2005, 7-Eleven was purchased by Seven and I Holdings Co., Ltd., in Tokyo, Japan and is run by 7-Eleven Japan.[19]

Why are franchises so successful? The franchiser understands its key customers, knows exactly what they want, and develops systems to deliver what its key customers want. The franchise system trains, manages, and regulates franchisees so they will consistently delight their key customers.

Imagine your distribution channels are franchisees and make sure they consistently delight your key customers.

> *"Your premium brand had better be delivering something special, or it's not going to get the business."*
> Warren [Edward] Buffett, business investor, CEO of
> Berkshire Hathaway, Inc., and philanthropist.

Apply Key #7: Deliver Delight to Your Key Customers.

What three or four distribution functions delight your key customers?

- Assortment
- Convenience
- Cost efficiency
- Financing
- Guarantees
- Insurance
- Packaging
- Personal service
- Point-of purchase information

- Quality control
- Reminders
- Shipping
- Social status
- Speed
- Store environment
- Technical support
- Training

Which of your distribution channels consistently delight your key customers?

Which distribution channels will be discontinued?

"Without promotion, something terrible happens—nothing!"
[Phineas Taylor] P. T. Barnum, founder of the Barnum
& Bailey Circus, author, 1810–1891.

CHAPTER 8

Promotion:
How to Promote

Patrick Is Not Another Carpet Cleaner.

Patrick is a carpet cleaner in a town full of carpet cleaners. "How can I promote my service when there are so many competitors?" He knows he cannot compete on price or his costs would drive him out of business. Some competitors brag their cleaning method is best. "Customers want clean carpets, not technology." Others rely upon referrals from their customers, but Patrick is just starting his business.

Patrick notices the carpet cleaner that specialized in hand-knotted rugs has gone out of business. These rugs require special handling. "I know how to clean hand-knotted rugs. Other carpet cleaners may ruin them."

Patrick visits stores in the area that sell hand-knotted rugs, gets acquainted with the owners, and leaves some business cards for referrals. "I can show them how to maintain the beauty of their rugs." The owners want to attract their customers to return to their stores so they schedule demonstrations for their customers. Before long, Patrick has a list of referrals from satisfied clients.

Who Believes a Conceited Ad?
An Aesop Tale

A businessman asks Aesop to evaluate some silly stuff he wrote to promote his business. Concerned about his boasting, the businessman says, "I hope you don't think that I am too presumptuous or too cocksure of my ability."

The man's wretched trash made Aesop sick. "I think you are quite right to praise yourself. You will never find anyone to do it for you."

Aesop conveys that an egotistical businessman is "his own trumpeter."

Trumpet Empathy with Your Key Customers.

Is your business its own trumpeter?

Many business owners are conceited. Some brag about their longevity, experience, or certificates. Others provide testimonials, list clients and projects, and display self-portraits. Egotistical business owners claim the broadest assortment, best service, highest customer satisfaction, and lowest prices.

Since only one competitor can be telling the truth, most prospects ignore such hyperbole. Do they really care about these boasts? No, prospects seek what brings them joy, fulfills their needs, or expresses their desired lifestyle. They want to solve their problems with your products and services.

Prospects want a hole, not a drill; a social group, not a twin-cam motorcycle; and glamour, not a stick of tinted wax. They care about the benefits and lasting value your business can provide them.

Should your business trumpet empathy?

Effective promotions are empathetic with your key customers and key prospects. Your promotions should provide the information your target market needs and convey it when, where, and how they need the information.

Your goal is to convey how your target market can solve their problems with your products and services. Discover what really matters to them. Walk in their moccasins, empathize with their desires, and understand their buying behavior. Mirror their feelings, visualize their success, and assist them with their purchase process.

How Valuable Is Empathy?

How do you evaluate promotional decisions?

You have many promotional decisions to make, but start with the most important decision. Then rank your options by their empathy with your target market and select the option that is most empathetic. This option will be the most effective choice (*Figure 9*).

Figure 9: Empathetic Promotions

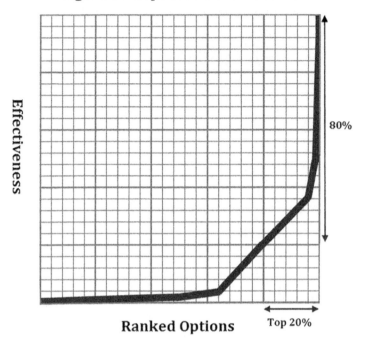

Ranked Options

Continue making promotional decisions based on their empathy with your target market. Then ask a representative group of your key customers to select their favorite promotion from a short list of possibilities.

Conveying empathy will satisfy your key customers, attract similar prospects to your business, and retain their loyalty. For example, Saturn owners still refer to their love for the brand.

Saturn Captured Our Hearts.

The advertising agency, Hal Riney & Partners (Riney), successfully introduced a new American automobile brand in June of 1990, to replace small, sporty Japanese automobiles:

No one had introduced a successful new brand in the automobile business [...] We built a whole new personality for customer belief. That folksy little company from Tennessee is an American car.[20]

Saturn asked Riney to make fundamental decisions:

We did everything [...] [Saturn] came to us one time and asked us, "What should we name it?" [...] "Just call it a Saturn coupe or a Saturn sedan and keep it simple" [...] "What do we call the colors, Sante Fe Sunset or what?" "How about "red?"[21]

Riney created a charismatic brand with the overarching message, "a different kind of car company; a different kind of car."

All you had to do was look at everything that Detroit did and just do the opposite, and that's virtually what we did. We guided the company through all that. It was extraordinarily rewarding to find out that this kind of honesty and straightforwardness and integrity that we tried to maintain, actually worked.[22]

Riney found ways to forge relationships with Saturn's customers:

Our job has not been to create commercials. Our job has been to solve problems [...] Our answer is to find ways to make people like this company and that took the form of letters we wrote to consumers and a thousand other things besides television commercials.[23]

According to Riney, early ads featured the first customers in a community telling others about their new Saturn and recommending they buy one:

> Saturn is great at using real customer stories in local commercials [...] People would rather do business with someone who has been recommended to them. Enthusiastic customers in commercials are effective in making those recommendations for you.[24] Typical is a recent regional commercial developed for cold-weather markets, touting how Saturn's traction-control system and anti-lock brakes handle winter driving conditions. The spot features Wisconsin resident, Jean Jubelirer, who drives her Saturn through snow to teach her Polynesian dance class.[25]

Customer satisfaction with Saturn was amazing. Saturn finished third, behind luxury brands Lexus and Infiniti.[26] Experts rated its brand management higher than luxury brands, Mercedes-Benz, Lexus, and BMW.[27]

Riney believed Saturn owners felt they belonged to a family:

> This summer we invited everyone who owned a Saturn to come and visit us in Tennessee, the place their car was born. We called it the Saturn Homecoming.

> People could see where their cars had been built and spend some time with the men and women who built them. They could see where the idea for a new kind of car company had taken shape. And we could thank them for believing we could do it.

Forty-four thousand people gave up their usual sum-
mer vacation to spend time with us at a car plant—a
pretty good turnout for our first big party [...] We were
all in it together, the way it's always been.[28]

Russ Hand, owner of two Saturn stores near Los Angeles,
California:

The advertising, marketing and positioning of the car
in the marketplace has been an unqualified success.
What's carrying Saturn is the perception it really is
"a different kind of company."[29]

Saturn's Vice President of Sales, Service, and Marketing, Joe
Kennedy:

We believe the enthusiasm that we have generated
amongst our customers has generated positive word
of mouth to an extraordinary extent, and *that*, more
than anything else, has fueled our sales success.[30]

Goodbye to my Saturn.

With great anticipation, I drove my Saturn toward a Humorous
Speech Contest of Toastmasters at a local university. My headlights
shone on the entrance to the campus. I stopped in the median to
cross the boulevard, but sea oats blocked my view of oncoming
traffic.

How could I escape this impasse? I rolled down my window
to listen for the sound of oncoming cars. I saw the light change
at the next intersection, noticing how the traffic flowed with the
light. The shadows lengthened into night.

Finally, I peeked around the sea oats and dashed across the street. An unlit car sped out of the darkness and smashed into my Saturn. A crowd gathered as I searched around the crushed glove box for my documents. My Saturn was totaled. Stunned, but unhurt, my tears flowed in grief for my beloved Saturn.

Key #8: Trumpet Empathy.

At what stage are your key prospects in their purchase process?

Are they gaining awareness, seeking options, comparing choices, making a decision, or timing their purchase? Learn about their purchase process by asking your key customers about their purchase process. What did they want to know and how did they feel at each stage in their search? Create promotion campaigns that will move your key prospects along to the next stage in their purchase process.

How can your business create an effective promotion?

Be empathetic when creating your promotion's headline, sub-head, copy, and call to action. Get inside your prospects' heads so you can speak to their emotions and use their "self-talk" to support your claims.

- Hook their attention with an emotional headline
- Clarify the benefit with the subhead
- Drive home the claims with the copy
- Motivate them with a call to action

Grab the attention of your key prospects with your graphics. Depict people who are similar to them or to their idealized self.

Dramatize their problem and demonstrate how your product or service will solve their problem. Use colors and symbols to convey their emotions.

You may wish to use a spokesperson to persuade your key prospects to buy your product or service. Who would influence them with this purchase? Is that person a celebrity, expert, sports hero, physician, or another high-profile person? Maybe your key prospects identify with a certain lifestyle or image of success. Which spokesperson best portrays what they want to achieve from using your offering?

How did your key customers seek information?

Discover which media vehicles facilitated and triggered their purchase decision.

- Searching the Internet

- Asking friends for recommendations

- Listening to a television or radio program

- Referring to a magazine, newspaper, e-zine, or blog

- Reading publicity

- Attending a special event

- Competing in a contest

- Responding to a direct marketing campaign

- Seeing a poster, sign, brochure, spec sheet, or display

- Evaluating products in a store

What event or passage in their life motivated their search process? What impelled them to buy your product or service? These answers determine where, when and how often you should schedule promotions for your key prospects.

Just like Saturn, decide to promote with empathy for key prospects of your business.

 Apply Key #8: Trumpet Empathy with Your Target Market.

Your key customers are similar to your key prospects, so seek to understand their buying behavior. Interview some key customers and probe for in-depth responses. Keep interviewing key customers until their responses become repetitive. They will predict the buying behavior of your key prospects and guide you to create empathetic promotions.

Interview Guide for Key Customers

Describe what instigated your purchase.

- Occasion
- Change in your life
- Observation

Describe factors that motivated your purchase.

- Emotion
- Need
- Desire

What information did you need at each stage of your purchase decision?

- Notice problem
- Identify options
- Compare options
- Decide to buy
- Time the purchase

How did you search for the information at each stage of your decision?

- People
- Media
- Stores

Describe the information that influenced you the most.

What were your requirements relative to features, reputation, and service?

What was the most important selection factor in your decision?

- Convenience
- Long-time value
- Relationship
- Image
- Price
- Uniqueness

Describe people and groups who influenced your decision.

What media informed you about the purchase?

- Blog
- Contest
- Display
- Event
- Magazine
- Radio
- E-zine
- Materials
- Television
- Internet search
- Newspaper
- Signage

Describe the options you considered.

- Competitors

- Other ways to solve the problem

How did you decide on your purchase?

- Convenience

- Impulse purchase

- Modeling another person

- Weighing alternatives

How long did you search for information?

Where did you shop for the item and where did you buy it?

What buying terms did you seek and receive?

What benefits did you want from the purchase and what did you receive?

How will the promotional campaign be empathetic with your target market and its search process?

CHAPTER 9

Prospecting: How to Target Prospects

Dinosaurs Devour the National Linen Service.

My first marketing research client was the National Linen Service (NLS) in Atlanta, Georgia. My client supplied and washed rolls of linen towels for restaurants, healthcare facilities, and industrial settings. In 1984, the vice president of marketing for NLS asked me to contrast current and past customers of their linen service.

Proudly, I brought him the research results and displayed them on his table. The vice president cued into one important fact—past customers had newer buildings than current customers. In anger, he shoved the results off the table. Noticing my shock, he said, "Our current customers are dinosaurs. No one but dinosaurs will want our service in the future. Without new prospects, we're going out of business!"

In 2013,[31] NLS was sold to Alsco, Inc., a worldwide industry leader with 120 service centers.

> Alsco provides a full line of professionally laundered linens delivered weekly for use in Food & Beverage, Healthcare and Industrial settings [...] We deliver only

the products you need, when you need them, freeing you to focus on your core business.[32]

The vice president of marketing for NLS believed that laundering rolls of linen towels was passé, but Alsco recognized and promoted its benefits to prospects.

What Teaches a Crab?
An Aesop Tale

An old crab criticizes her son. "Why do you walk sideways like that, my son, and rub your sides against the wet rock? You ought to walk straight."

Sweetly, the young crab replied, "Since you want to teach me, show me how to walk straight, my dear mother, and I'll follow your example."

The old crab tries, but she tries in vain. "I was foolish to find fault with you."

Aesop says, "Example is better than precept."

Ways to Identify Key Prospects.

Are key customers examples of your key prospects?

Was Aesop right—do we learn best by example? Can your key customers predict who will be your key prospects? Many direct marketing companies can use the traits of the top twenty percent of your customers to identify your key prospects.

For example, the Advanced Customer Cloner by InfoUSA can target prospects in the United States and Canada. "We'll analyze your customers to find hot prospects just like them!"[33] You can use one trait or several traits of your key customers to target your key prospects. Let's see what traits InfoUSA has available to target businesses and consumers.

How can InfoUSA identify key business prospects?

InfoUSA compiles information about seventeen million businesses. Its sources include Yellow Page directories, government sources, annual reports, press releases, and websites. For example, a government building project manager can identify minority roofing contractors with at least fifty employees. Maybe your business seeks distributors that spend at least a million dollars on travel. Another example is to target growing retail businesses in the Chicago metropolitan area.

How can InfoUSA identify your key consumer prospects?

On a monthly basis, InfoUSA updates information for about 230 million consumers from 100 different sources. For example, do you seek young women who recently bought a home in your area? Is your target market mail-order buyers who subscribe to a car magazine? Maybe your key prospects are rich diabetics. Are you targeting major donors whose social group is "Big Fish, Small Pond."[34] InfoUSA can also identify unemployed graduates in mass communication who spend hours on the Internet and buy many electronics.

What Are the Three Steps to Higher Profits?

The first step is to describe your key customers. According to the 80/20 rule, the most profitable 20 percent of your customers will generate 80 percent of your profits *(Figure 10)*.

The second step is to deliver delight to your key customers with your products and services. Decide to discontinue promotions to your other customers. Quit wasting resources by promoting to the 80 percent of your customers who only generate 20 percent of your profits *(Figure 11)*.

The third step is to promote to prospects who are similar to your key customers. They will be easy to convert into highly profitable new customers. When they replace the customers you lost, your business will multiply its profits 5-fold (100% / 20% = 5) *(Figure 12)*.

Describe Key Customers

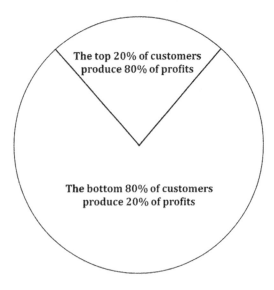

The top 20% of customers produce 80% of profits

The bottom 80% of customers produce 20% of profits

Figure 11: Delight Key Customers

Delight your key
customers

Figure 12: Convert Prospects Into Customers

When all customers are
highly profitable, your
profits increase five-fold.

An example of the 80/20 rule.

My beautician is a young woman with deep purple hair and an eyebrow stud. Jessica worked for J. C. Penney's Beauty Salon in Volusia Mall, Daytona Beach, Florida. Each year Jessica beautified around a thousand regulars and walk-in shoppers and they averaged four visits per year. After subtracting her overhead, Jessica earned roughly ten dollars per head so her annual income was around forty thousand dollars per year *(Table 4)*.

Table 4: Steps in Targeting Key Prospects

	Clients	Average Visits	Total Visits	Profit
Penney's Salon	1000	4	4000	$40,000
Beautiful Salon, Year 1	800	1	800	$8,000
Beautiful Salon, Year 2	1600	2.5	4000	$40,000

Every August, Penney's "back-to-school" promotion offered children free haircuts and paid the beauticians a pittance for their work. Jessica whispered to me, "I hate to cut their tangled manes. The kids challenge my patience, pre-empt my regulars, and cut my profits." She vowed to never again cope with Penney's "back-to-school" promotion.

Jessica moved her business to Beautiful Salon & Day Spa in Ormond Beach, Florida, an owner-managed salon in an upscale mall. About 80% of her clients (80% × 1000 = 800) followed Jessica to the Beautiful Salon, but they produced roughly 20% of her profits at Penney's Salon (20% × $40,000 = $8,000). In her first year at the Beautiful Salon, Jessica earned around eight thousand dollars.

The other 20% (20% × 1000 = 200) were employees of J. C. Penney's or were frequent patrons of the store. They averaged 16 visits per year and produced about 80% of her profits at Penney's (80% × $40,000 = $32,000).

Disappointed, Jessica identified the most profitable 20% of her remaining clients (20% × 800 = 160). They averaged four visits per year and produced roughly 80% of her profits (80% × $8,000 = $6,400). She knew her other clients would visit her sporadically and would only produce around 20% of her profits (20% × $8,000 = $1,600).

She offered her key clients a discount for referring their friends to her. They and their friends attracted eight hundred highly profitable new clients. Just like her key clients, they averaged four visits a year and produced generous profits (800 × 4 × $10 = $32,000). Soon Jessica was earning around forty thousand dollars per year.

Key #9: Target Key Prospects.

Emery-Riddle Aeronautical University (ERAU) soars.

ERAU educates students at residential campuses in Daytona Beach, Florida and Prescott, Arizona, and through more than 150 locations in the United States, Europe, Asia, Canada and the Middle East. ERAU expects to double in size by 2020 and is spending around $250 million to prepare for the influx of aviation enthusiasts at its headquarters in Daytona Beach. "Embry-Riddle Aeronautical University is the world's largest, fully accredited university specializing in aviation and aerospace."[35]

> This school is best suited for aviation enthusiasts—
> people that want to pursue a career in aviation business, management, engineering, air traffic control, and piloting.[36]

Evidently, its key prospects are college-prep high school students who are aviation enthusiasts from around the world. Currently

ERAU offers a $1,000 per year scholarship to students who are referred by alumni. There are many other ways ERAU could identify key prospects.

- Solicit referrals from InfoUSA's list of Airplane Owners and Pilots.

- Use InfoUSA's Advanced Customer Cloner to match the top 20% of its students with prospects in the United States and Canada.

- Contact teenage members of the Academy of Model Aeronautics (AMA) clubs and participants in its model competitions.[37]

- Contact teenage members of the Experimental Aircraft Association (EAA) chapters around the world.[38]

- Collect contact information from high school students who attend air shows. For example, the EAA sponsors AirVenture Oshkosh, one of the largest air shows in the world. One of its performance teams is Wings and Waves from ERAU.[39]

You can learn from this example how to target key prospects of your business with a direct marketing campaign.

*"In marketing I've seen only one strategy that can't miss—
and that is to market to your best customers first,
your best prospects second, and the rest of the world last."*
John Romero, video game designer, co-founder of Id Software.

Apply Key #9: Target Key Prospects Similar to Your Key Customers.

If targeting key business clients, describe a few of their most important traits from this list of possibilities:

- Type of business: SIC or NAICS code, Yellow Page heading, and sales volume

- Category of business: new, home-based, small, growing, big, or bankrupt

- Management: gender, ethnicity, title, occupation, profession, and ownership

- Spending: credit rating, computers, and other business expenses by category

- Other information: location, longevity, number of employees, and brand

If targeting key consumers, describe a few of their most important traits from this list of possibilities:

- Household: socioeconomic status, housing, investments, and donations

- Spending: vehicles, electronics, other expenses, and credit card use

- Residents: gender, age, ethnicity, religion, income, insurance, or occupation

- Major event: new home owners, college students by field, and bankruptcy

- Usage: subscriptions, medications, mail ordering, and online activities

- Lifestyle: opinions, interests, hobbies, and social group

What traits will your business use to target key prospects with direct marketing?

CHAPTER 10

Customer Service: How to Set Policy

Accounting for Failure.

At a luncheon I sat next to the manager of a CPA firm and mentioned the 80/20 rule. She exclaimed, "Long ago we realized the 80/20 rule predicts our sales so our sales reps seek prospects who are similar to our most profitable clients." I asked, "How do you describe them?" Dodging, she replied, "Many CPA firms are chasing the same clients." "What special benefits do you provide your top clients?" "We treat our clients equally."

I asked her, "What about complainers?" "We're going through a difficult time so we don't want to lose any clients. We do whatever it takes to keep complainers from switching to a competitor." Speechless from her flawed logic, I thought, "That's why you're going through a difficult time."

Can a Soldier Ride a Donkey?
An Aesop Tale

A soldier feeds his horse well on barley when they are at war. The horse says, "We share our dangers and adventures."

When the war is over, the horse says, "You make me work like a slave. I must carry heavy loads and get nothing to eat but chaff."

The trumpet sounds the call to arms. The soldier bridles the horse, arms himself, and mounts, but the horse has no strength.

Stumbling at every step, the horse says, "You better go join an infantry regiment for I'm no longer worth riding with the cavalry. You changed me into a donkey. How can you expect to change me back into a horse?"

Aesop notes that a soldier cannot ride a donkey into battle to "save us in the time of trouble."

Do Not Neglect Your Key Customers.

Aesop warns us against neglecting an important asset like a soldier's horse. Most sales people wine and dine prospects during the sales process, but ignore them when they become key customers.

When a business raises its prices, neglected customers may lose interest and switch to a competitor. "I'm no longer your customer since I'm buying from a competitor. How can you expect me to return?"

A wise business rewards its key customers so they will remain loyal when they raise their prices. Your key customers deserve to be rewarded since they produce 80 percent of your profits and refer key prospects to your business.

Does your business reward key customers or neglect them? Most businesses neglect their key customers and give special attention to complainers, but you can increase your profits by doing the reverse.

Complainers are in the bottom 80 percent of customers so they produce little profit. As my grandmother said, "The squeaky wheel gets the grease." They complain because your business does not fulfill their requirements.

Obviously, complainers believe that a competitor can better meet their needs. Maybe a competitor specializes in serving people just like them. Why not encourage them to switch to a competitor?

Discourage complainers by stratifying your customer service policies according to relevant criteria. Your business is not discriminating against complainers if you are being consistent with your policies. Provide perks to your key customers, but limit your benefits to other customers. Reward your key customer as they reward your business.

How Much Trouble Can Complainers Cause?

My condominium suffered from complainers.

In 2004, the Pendleton Condominium suffered from a "time of trouble" when four hurricanes, Charley, Frances, Jeanne, and Ivan, slammed into Daytona Beach, Florida. Originally, the 127 condominiums had screened balconies, but most owners installed windowpanes in the flimsy frames. The hurricanes buckled the frames, sucked out panes, and pierced the ground with shards of glass.

After the hurricanes, the owners replaced the glass, but a few years later, the board voted for an assessment to enclose our balconies with hurricane-proof glass. Some owners complained about the decision. Twenty-five households (20% × 127 = 25) made about 80% of the complaints.

Five of the households ($20\%^2$ × 127 = 5) made almost two-thirds of the complaints ($80\%^2$ = 64%) and became a public nuisance. They jammed the office of the local building code chief for several days. "The condominium cannot force us to pay the assessment!" One household ($20\%^3$ × 127 = 1) made over half of the complaints ($80\%^3$ = 51%) and threatened to sue the association *(Figure 13)*.

Figure 13: Complainers

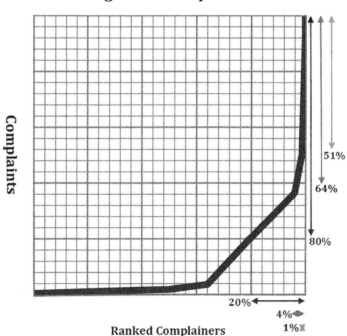

The president of the board of directors waited for everyone to agree to the assessment. Meanwhile, the owners could not obtain building permits to improve their units for sale. "During the delay, the housing bubble burst and I got caught owning two units."

The impasse was resolved when the local building code chief decided that putting glass in screen frames was against building code. This decision quieted the complainers and the board assessed the owners for the project.

As a result of the assessment, the owners added a window wall overlooking the Halifax River and more than a hundred square feet of air conditioned living area. Once the project was completed, all owners were delighted with the results.

Key #10: Reward the Best.

For many years Mr. Iocco, CPA, CIC, was a regional executive vice president of Brown & Brown Insurance, one of the largest independent insurance agencies in the United States. While at Brown & Brown, Mr. Iocco was responsible for hundreds of sales executives who collectively produced more than five hundred million dollars of insurance premiums in the northeastern region.

"Brown & Brown taught its sales representatives to focus on personally servicing the most profitable twenty percent of its customers." Mr. Iocco stratified the customer service policy for offices in his region by automating routine interactions with the other eighty percent of customers. Although this policy seemed capricious to some sales executives, Mr. Iocco noticed the top 20% of his customers consistently produced 80% of his region's sales and profits.

Step one.

Mr. Iocco became tired of traveling throughout his region, left his position, and decided to work out of his elegant country home near Charlotte, North Carolina. He combined insurance agencies in Bristol, Norton, Richlands, and Salem, Virginia, into Trustpoint Insurance and became its managing partner. Trustpoint offers personal auto, homeowners, business, and benefits insurance. Initially, Trustpoint treated customers equally *(Table 5)*.

Table 5: An Example of Sales Commissions

Step	Clients	% of Sales	Results	Pay Rate	Sales (000)	Pay (000)
1	100%	100%	1-fold	20%	$100	$20
2a	20%	80%	4-fold	20%	$80	$16
2b	20%	80%	4-fold	25%	$100	$20
3	100%	400%	4-fold	25%	$400	$100

Step two.

Mr. Iocco stratified the customer service policy at Trustpoint Insurance like offices in his region of Brown & Brown Insurance. The policy rewarded the most profitable twenty percent of the customers with personally delivered value-added services and automated routine interactions with other customers.

The sales reps complained that taking away 80% of their customers would lower their personal income. Mr. Iocco obtained buy in from the sales team by increasing their sales commission pay rate from 20% to 25%.

Step three.

The sales reps discovered they could earn the same commission from a fifth of their previous customers. "We need to work only one day a week." On the other four days, the sales reps went hunting—for new customers to replace the customers they had lost.

The sales reps identified prospects that were similar to the most profitable twenty percent of Trustpoint's customers. They converted most of these key prospects into highly profitable new customers. Like the key customers, the new customers produced 4-fold results. Mr. Iocco was not surprised because the 80/20 rule predicts these results.

> Throughout my years of selling and servicing insurance, the results were exactly as Dr. Kruger predicts in her book. In both the large and small businesses, 80% of our revenue and business profit came from the top 20% of our customers.

Steps four and five.

Some sales reps focus on the top 4% of Trustpoint's customers ($20\%^2$) and seek prospects just like them. These customers produce 16-fold commissions (4^2). A few sales reps focus on the top .8% of Trustpoint's customers ($20\%^3$) because they expect to produce 64-fold commissions (4^3).

Learn from Robert Iocco how to reward your most profitable customers and discourage complainers. Decide to stratify the customer service policy of your business.

> *"The best customer service is if the customer doesn't need to call you, doesn't need to talk to you. It just works."*
> Jeff Bezos [Jeffrey Preston Jorgesen], founder of
> Amazon.com, investor, and technology entrepreneur.

 ## Apply Key #10: Stratify Your Customer Service Policy.

How can your business reward its best customers?

- Personal value-added services

- Better products and services

- Volume discounts

- Faster service and shipping

- Free training and support

- Free insurance and guarantees

- Automatic reordering

- Recognition and prestige

- Reports, autographs, and trinkets

- Influence with future decisions

How can your business discourage less profitable customers and complainers?

- Automate routine interactions with less profitable customers and complainers

- Re-define your target market to exclude customers with these traits

- Only accept returns with a receipt or in exchange for a similar item

- Establish other rigid procedures that discourage less profitable customers and complainers

How will your business reward key customers and discourage complainers?

"If money follows results, we will get more results for our money."
Bob Riley, race car designer and co-founder of Riley Technologies.

CHAPTER 11

Budgeting: How to Allocate Money

Trade Your Talents.

Did Aesop influence Jesus who lived several centuries later? This is how I interpret his parable of the talents.

> A man entrusts his wealth to three servants while he travels. Two servants trade his talents to increase the man's wealth. The third servant digs a hole in the ground and hides the wealth. When the man returns, he praises the two successful businessmen but condemns the unprofitable miser.[40]

What Use is a Miser's Gold?
An Aesop Tale

Aesop's neighbor converted all of his riches into gold, melted it into an ingot, and buried it in a secret place. Every day he gloated over his treasure for hours. Aesop said, "He left his heart and spirit in the hole."

His servant snoops on him, sneaks back to the place, and snitches the lump of gold. When the miser returns, he discovers the hole is empty. In despair, the man pulls his hair and cries, "My treasure is gone!"

Aesop sympathizes with his neighbor's loss. "Don't despair like that, my friend. You won't miss it. Just put a brick in the hole and imagine it's your gold. You won't be any worse off than before. Before you lost it, your gold was of no earthly use to you."

Aesop chides misers. "Unused possessions create no good."

Make Good Use of Your Wealth.

Both Aesop and Jesus encourage you to use your wealth for good, instead of hoarding it. Your business can provide benefits to your customers, income to your employees, and profits to yourself.

What is the cost of losing an opportunity?

Opportunity cost is the amount your business could have profited from an opportunity. If you act on an opportunity, your business will produce profits. If you do not act on an opportunity, your business will suffer an opportunity cost that will not appear in its accounting records. A wise entrepreneur evaluates the profitability of various opportunities and selects the one that promises the best profits.

Key #11: Concentrate Resources.

Constance, the owner of a business, wants to roll the budget over to the next year, but Dwight, her marketing consultant, disagrees. "Your business should invest its money where it will earn the best profit. If your business focuses on serving its key customers, its profits will multiply. The top twenty percent of its customers will produce sixteen times more profits than its other customers."

Confused, she asks, "Where will my business find the money?"

"Your business can quit spending money on less profitable customers. Let's start with the mission of your business. Its most profitable customers demand high-quality products and services so focus on quality. Less profitable customers prefer cheaper versions that dilute the reputation of your business."

"How can my business improve its reputation?"

"Your business has a stellar reputation in its strength. Compete on this strength and help others compensate for a weakness. Likewise, your business can delegate its weaknesses to suppliers, so your business can specialize in its strength. Your business should contract with professionals, specialists, and service companies. What benefits do you provide and who really benefits from them?"

Constance describes its key customers and how her business benefits them. "Your business offers treasures to its most profitable customers, but why does it offer product and services that generate little profit?"

"Maybe my business should discontinue less profitable items and add value to products and services that are treasured by its key customers."

"How much profit would you lose if your business charges more than its direct competitor?"

"The bottom eighty percent of its customers would switch to the competitor, but my business would only lose twenty percent of its profits. Increasing the price would greatly increase our profit per item. The overall effect would be a large increase in our total profits."

"Which distributors and retailers consistently delight your key customers?"

Constance lists them and says, "Some others tarnish our reputation and cause more problems than they're worth. Maybe my business should consider some new distribution channels."

"Your promotions seem to focus on all customers, not the top twenty percent of your customers. Your promotions must trumpet empathy with its key customers. Your key customers have different motivations, timing, media usage, and influences than your other customers. Let's evaluate your direct marketing campaign. Does it currently target your key prospects?"

"No, we should focus on results, not reach."

"Why does your business reward complainers?"

"I was taught in school to treat everyone equally."

"Does everyone treat your business equally? Reward the best, not the rest. I have brought up many ways your business can allocate money to its key customers and away from its other customers. Focus where your business will get the best profits. Don't feel overwhelmed. Just make one decision at a time. Decisions are useless until your business acts on them. The 80/20 rule is an engine that can power your prosperity. Your budget will ignite the engine so your decisions will jump into action." Dwight shakes her hand and cordially leaves her office.

That night Constance dreams about the bedtime story, *The Little Engine That Could.* In her dream she chants, "I know I can, I know I can, I know I can." She visualizes the 80/20 rule as the engine of her business, building momentum and chugging upward at an ever-accelerating pace.

Does this story inspire you to concentrate your resources on serving the key customers and other top inputs of your business?

"Prune—prune businesses, products,
activities, people. Do it annually."
Donald Rumsfeld, Secretary of Defense under George W. Bush and Gerald Ford.

 Apply Key #11: Concentrate Business Resources on Top Inputs.

How can your business alter its budget to improve the quality of its products and services?

- Buy higher quality components

- Sell inferior areas of your business

- Reward and nurture high-quality employees

How can your business alter its budget to specialize in its strengths?

- Expand buildings and equipment to produce the specialty of your business

- Sell assets that produce other products and services

- Hire and train employees in this specialty

- Outplace employees whose skills are not compatible with its specialty

How can your business alter its budget to delegate its weaknesses?

- Outsource weaknesses in functions, projects, and responsibilities to suppliers

- Contract with relevant professionals, specialists, and service companies

- Build strategic alliances with suppliers who compensate for your weaknesses

How can your business alter its budget to focus on its key customers?

- List the top 20 percent of its customers and profile their typical traits

- Conduct marketing research so your company better understands its key customers

- Delegate other customers to competitors that can better serve them

How can your business alter its budget to offer treasures to key customers?

- Research what benefits and values that key customers want from its offerings

- Add value to products and services that are treasured by key customers

- Discontinue products and services for other customers

How can your business project improve its revenue from key customers?

- Identify the price at which its key customers would switch to a competitor

- Gradually raise the price near this price point

- Gain in profit margin what is lost in profits from eighty percent of the customers

How can your business alter its budget to consistently delight its key customers?

- Reward distributors and retailers that delight key customers of your business

- Discontinue contracts and agreements with other distribution channels

- Find new distributors and retailers who can consistently delight its key customers

How can your business alter its promotional budget to empathize with key customers?

- Research the process your key customers used in deciding to buy your offerings

- Target key customers and prospects with promotions, spokespeople, and publicity

- Quit targeting other customers with its promotional budget

How can your business alter its budget to target top prospects with direct marketing?

- Research how to best influence top prospects with a direct marketing campaign

- Use a list of key prospects from a direct marketing business like InfoUSA

- Discontinue direct marketing campaigns that target other prospects and customers

How can your business alter its budget to reward key customers, rather than complainers?

- Stratify your customer service policy to reward key customers

- Discontinue benefits to less profitable customers and complainers

- Encourage top complainers to switch to a competitor

How will your business allocate resources to implement these strategic marketing decisions?

CHAPTER 12

Taking Action: How to Spark Profits

Your Mentor is Proud of You.

Two months later the two distributors meet again at Starbucks to enjoy their lattes. The novice gushes about her latest endeavors and the mentor displays an award that names her as the "Most Valuable Distributor." They don't notice that Aesop is looking over their shoulders.

After summarizing their last two months of business activities, her mentor asks, "How is your prospecting coming along?"

Confidently, the novice shows her a short list of prospects. "I've learned that quality, not quantity counts."

Pleased, her mentor asks, "How did you prune your list?"

"Instead of frantically chasing prospects, I calmly analyzed my key customers. I know that haste makes waste."

"How did you analyze them?"

"I'm skilled in sales, not analysis. I was too lazy to analyze them myself. I'll go further by using my own gift."

"Who helped you?"

"A friend imported my customer database into Excel, calculated their profitability, and put them in sequential order. I offered to refer him to others if he would do the analysis for me. I'm as good as my word."

"Did you interview the most profitable twenty percent of your customers?"

"Yes, I wanted to be able to empathize with them. I'll use different strokes for different folks."

"What surprised you?"

"I didn't realize how much my customers value our products and services. Maybe we should raise our prices. After all, utility is the test of worth."

"What else did you learn?"

"Their purchase process involves so many people. I must consistently follow up so their purchases are not diverted by their procedures. The process is slow but sure."

"Did the interviews change your approach to sales?"

"Yes, I'll be more empathetic and quit trumpeting about our products and services."

"Did the traits of your key customers help you identify your key prospects?"

"I profiled my top customers and eliminated all prospects who did not fit the profile. Their example was my precept."

"What about complainers?"

"Most companies reward complainers for complaining. Instead, I refer complainers to a competitor that can better serve them. I reward customers as they reward my business. My key customers can save me in a time of trouble."

"Were you able to convert key prospects into highly profitable customers?"

"Oh, yes. I spent money promoting to my key prospects so it's easy to convert them into new customers. Unused possessions create no good."

The mentor dashes off to an appointment as the novice sips her latte. Looking up, she notices Aesop. "Your insights made all the difference. You mean so much to me." With a nod of his head, Aesop vanishes into thin air.

What Proves the Truth?
An Aesop Tale

A man practices jumping, racing, wrestling, and throwing the javelin for the Pentathlon, but his fellow citizens consider him unmanly. The man escapes their teasing by traveling abroad.

When the man returns, he boasts about performing remarkable feats in various countries. He brags that his long jump in Rhodes was better than the winner of the Olympic Games. "Just go to Rhodes and ask them. Everyone will tell you it's true."

A bystander says, "If you can jump that well, we needn't go to Rhodes to prove it. Let's just imagine for a moment this is Rhodes and now—jump!"

Aesop reminds us that talk is superfluous when we can prove the truth by taking action. He encourages "deeds, not words."

Prove the 80/20 Rule by Jumping into Action.

The bystander challenges the traveler to prove the truth of his boast by jumping. Likewise, I challenge you to prove the 80/20 rule by jumping into action with your business. For example, the predictions of the 80/20 rule seem like empty boasts, but you can prove their truth by taking action.

You made key marketing decisions that prioritize the top inputs of your business. For example, you strategically decided to focus on quality, compete on strength, delegate weaknesses, and describe key customers. You specifically decided to offer treasures, price as valued, deliver delight, and trumpet empathy. Finally, you operationally decided to target key prospects, reward the best, concentrate resources, and jump into action.

When combined, these twelve key marketing decisions encompass all components of a strategic marketing plan. Each of your decisions applies the 80/20 rule to your business and clarifies how your business can multiply its profits.

How Can Your Business Magnify Its Profits?

Most examples show how to multiply your profits by focusing on the top twenty percent of your customers. *Table 6* shows how to magnify your profits by focusing on higher layers of your customers.

Table 6: Layers of the 80/20 Rule

Layer	Top Inputs	Top Outputs	Results	Bottom Inputs	Bottom Outputs	Ratio
1	20%	80%	4-fold (80/20)	80%	20%	16 (4/.25)
2	4% $(20\%^2)$	64% $(80\%^2)$	16-fold (4^2)	96%	36%	256 (16^2)
3	.8% $(20\%^3)$	51% $(80\%^3)$	64-fold (4^3)	99.2%	49%	4096 (16^3)
4	.16% $(20\%^4)$	41% $(80\%^4)$	256-fold (4^4)	99.84%	59%	65,536 (16^4)

Dr. Ben Carson Interviews A. G. Gaston

Dr. Ben Carson, retired Director of Pediatric Neurosurgery at Johns Hopkins Medical Institutions, interviewed A. G. Gaston, a major contributor to the civil rights movement in the South. "Mr. Gaston, how did you as a black man become a multimillionaire in Birmingham, Alabama, in the 1930s to 1950s?"

"It's very simple. I just opened my eyes, looked around, and asked myself, what do people need? I then went about fulfilling those needs."[41]

 ### Apply Key #12: Jump into Action with Your Decisions.

How did you answer the questions at the end of each chapter?

- The mission of your business is to offer what high-quality products and services?

- What is the unique strength of your business?

- What specific functions, tasks, and projects will your business delegate to relevant suppliers?

- What are the typical traits of your key customers on relevant aspects of their demographics, lifestyle, and buying behavior?

- How will your business improve the value of products and services for your key customers and which items will be discontinued?

- How much will your key customers pay for the products and services they treasure?

- Which distribution channels consistently delight your key customers and which ones will be discontinued?

- How will the promotional campaign be empathetic with your target market and its search process?

- What traits will your business use to target key prospects with direct marketing?

- How will your customer service policies reward key customers and discourage complainers?

- How will your business allocate resources to implement these strategic marketing decisions?

- Who will implement these decisions and specifically how will this occur?

Combine your answers into a strategic marketing plan for your business.

Key #12: Jump into Action.

Congratulations, Fellow Traveler, for completing *Aesop's Keys to Profitable Marketing* and deciding how to apply the 80/20 rule to your business. Prove the profitability of your marketing decisions and now—jump into action.

"It is in your moments of decision that your destiny is shaped."
[Anthony] Tony Robbins, peak performance coach, consultant, and author.

Endnotes

1   Robert and Olivia Temple, *The Complete Fables: Aesop* (London: Penguin Classics, 1998).

2   Vilfredo Pareto, *Cours d'economie politique* [Course in political economy] (Lausanne, Switzerland: Rouge, 1896–7).

3   Myers-Briggs Foundation, http://www.myersbriggs.org/my-mbti-personality-type/mbti-basics

4   "Daytona State Music Student Earns Top Honors at Symposium," *Daytona Times: East Central Florida's Black Voice* (February 20, 2014).

5   Frank Kern, *The New Money Masters: How a Surfer and Family Man Started with Nothing and Learned to Generate $23.8 Million in 24 hours* (San Diego, CA: Robbins Research International, Inc., 2009), DVD.

6   Frank Kern, blog, http://www.masscontrolsite.com/blog/?p=57

7   Elizabeth Kruger, "Substantiating the Comparative Advantage Theory," *Proceedings*, Decision Science Institute Annual Meeting, San Antonio, TX (November 18–21, 2006).

8   Mark E. J. Newman, "Power lLaws, Pareto Distributions, and Zipf's aw," *Contemporary Physics 46*, 323–351 (January 2005).

9   Malcolm Gladwell, *Blink: The Power of Thinking without Thinking* (New York: Little, Brown, 2005).

[10] Bruce W. McCalley, *Model T Ford: The Car That Changed the World* (Iola, WI, 1994), http://www.oldcarsbookstore.com/model-t-ford-car-that-changed-world?

[11] Daniel Henninger, "Taking Cain Seriously," *The Wall Street Journal* (September 29, 2011).

[12] Ibid.

[13] Richard Lee, blog, http://www.deskeng.com/articles/aabpbf.htm

[14] Bluebeam, website, http://www.bluebeam.com/us/bluebeam-difference

[15] "Saturn's No Haggle Policy," commercial, www.youtube.com/watch?v=HZ41GNBHHzs

[16] "2012 Top 100 Retailers," *Stores*, http://www.stores.org/2012/Top-100-Retailers

[17] "Wal-Mart Rolling Out New Company Slogan," *Reuters* (September 12, 2007).

[18] "Top 10 Franchisers," http://en.wikipedia.org/wiki/Franchising

[19] 7-Eleven Japan, website, http://www.sej.co.jp/company/en/history.html

[20] "Riney on Saturn," *Independent Lens*, http://www.youtube.com/watch?v=ui1hXWmJpBI

[21] Ibid.

[22] Ibid.

[23] Ibid.

[24] Vicki Lenz, *The Saturn Difference: Creating Customer Loyalty in Your Company* (New York: John Wiley & Sons, 1990), 90–91.

[25] "Saturn Commercial," 1995, http://www.youtube.com/watch?v=FHFoc9UkLpQ

26   J. D. Power & Associates, *1994 Customer Satisfaction Index* (Agoura Hills, CA).

27   Ibid., 91.

28   "Saturn Homecoming," commercial, http://www.youtube.com/watch?v=KHpSsf9AeJU

29   Ibid.

30   Lenz, 250.

31   Indeed, job directory, website, http://www.indeed.com/cmp/National-Linen-Service/reviews

32   Yellowpages, directory, http://www.yellowpages.com/atlanta-ga/mip/alsco-20636380

33   InfoUSA, website, http://ca.infousa.com/ca/default.aspx

34   Claritas, Prizm market segments, The Nielsen Company, http://www.claritas.com/MyBestSegments/Default.jsp?ID=30

35   Wings and Waves, website, http://www.wingsandwaves.com/news/

36   Emery-Riddle Aeronautical University, website, http://www.campusdiscovery.com/colleges/profile/embry-riddle-aeronautical-university-daytona-beach-campus#reviews

37   Academy of Model Aeronautics, website, http://www.modelaircraft.org/

38   Experimental Aircraft Association, website, https://secure.eaa.org/apps/joinrenew/join.aspx?sc=219

39   Wings and Waves, website, http://www.wingsandwaves.com/news/

40   Matthew 25:14–29, *NRSV*.

41   Carson, Ben, *America the Beautiful: Rediscovering What Made This Nation Great* (Grand Rapids, MI: Zondervan, 2012), 76.

Bibliography

"2012 Top 100 Retailers." *Stores*, http://www.stores.org/2012/ Top-100-Retailers.

7-Eleven Japan, website, http://www.sej.co.jp/company/en/history .html

Experimental Aircraft Association, website, https://secure.eaa .org/apps/joinrenew/join.aspx?sc=219

Bluebeam, website, http://www.bluebeam.com/us/bluebeam-difference

Carson, Ben. *America the Beautiful: Rediscovering What Made This Nation Great*. Grand Rapids, MI: Zondervan, 2012.

Claritas, Prizm market segments, The Nielsen Company, http://www.claritas.com/MyBestSegments/Default.jsp?ID=30

"Daytona State Music Student Earns Top Honors at Symposium." *Daytona Times: East Central Florida's Black Voice*, February 20, 2014.

Emery-Riddle Aeronautical University, website, http://www .campusdiscovery.com/colleges/profile/embry-riddle-aeronautical-university-daytona-beach-campus#reviews

Academy of Model Aeronautics, website, http://www.model aircraft.org/

Gladwell, Malcolm. Blink: *The Power of Thinking without Thinking*. New York: Little, Brown, 2005.

Henninger, Daniel. "Taking Cain Seriously." *The Wall Street Journal*, September 29, 2011.

Indeed, job directory, website http://www.indeed.com/cmp/
National-Linen-Service/reviews

InfoUSA, website, http://ca.infousa.com/ca/default.aspx

J. D. Power & Associates. *1994 Customer Satisfaction Index.*
Agoura Hills, CA.

Kern, Frank, blog, http://www.masscontrolsite.com/blog/?p=57

Kern, Frank. *The New Money Masters: How a Surfer and Family
Man Started with Nothing and Learned to Generate $23.8
Million in 24 hours,* San: Diego, CA: Robbins Research
International, Inc., 2009, DVD.

Koch, Richard. *The 80/20 Principle: The Secret to Achieving More
with Less.* New York: Doubleday, 2008.

_____. *The Breakthrough Principle of 16x: Real Simple Innovation
for 16 Times Better Results.* Dallas, TX: Pritchett Publishing
Group, 2006.

Kruger, Elizabeth. "Substantiating the Comparative Advantage
Theory." *Proceedings, Decision Science Institute Annual
Meeting, San Antonio, TX,* November 18–21, 2006.

Lee, Richard, blog, http://www.deskeng.com/articles/aabpbf.htm

Lenz, Vicki. *The Saturn Difference: Creating Customer Loyalty in
Your Company.* New York: John Wiley & Sons, 1999.

Marshall, Perry. *80/20 Sales and Marketing: The Definitive Guide
to Working Less and Making More.* Irvine, CA: Entrepreneur
Press. 2013.

Matthew 25:14–29. NRSV

McCalley, Bruce W. *Model T Ford: The Car That Changed the
World.* Iola, WI, 1994, http://www.oldcarsbookstore.com/
model-t-ford-car-that-changed-world?

Myers-Briggs Foundation. http://www.myersbriggs.org/my-mbti-
personality-type/mbti-basics/

Newman, Mark E. J. "Power Laws, Pareto Distributions, and Zipf's Law." *Contemporary Physics* 46 (January 2005): 323–351.

Pareto, Vilfredo. Cours d'economie politique [Course in political economy]. Lausanne, Switzerland: Rouge, 1896–7.

"Riney on Saturn." *Independent Lens*, http://www.youtube.com/watch?v=ui1hXWmJpBI

"Saturn Commercial." 1995, http://www.youtube.com/watch?v=FHFoc9UkLpQ

"Saturn Homecoming." commercial, http://www.youtube.com/watch?v=KHpSsf9AeJU

"Saturn's No Haggle Policy," commercial, www.youtube.com/watch?v=HZ41GNBHHzs

Temple, Robert and Olivia Temple. *The Complete Fables: Aesop.* London: Penguin Classics, 1998.

"Top 10 Franchisers." http://en.wikipedia.org/wiki/franchising

"Walmart Rolling Out New Company Slogan." *Reuters*, September 12, 2007.

Wings and Waves, website, http://www.wingsandwaves.com/news/

Yellowpages Directory, website, http://www.yellowpages.com/atlanta-ga/mip/alsco-20636380

Index

7-Eleven Japan, 70

Academy of Model Aeronautics, 92
AirVenture Oshkosh, 92
Alsco, Inc., 85–86
amazon.com, Inc., 102
American Machine and Foundry
    (AMF, Inc.), 33
Apple, Inc., 60, 62

Barnum & Bailey Circus, 72
Barnum, P. T., 72
Bastiat, Frederic, 22
Beautiful Salon & Day Spa, 90–91
Berkshire Hathaway, Inc., 70
Bernhardt, Ken, iii
Bethune-Cookman University,
    49–50
Bezos, Jeff, 102
Bluebeam Software, Inc., 47–48,
    50, 55
Bombardier Recreational
    Products, 48–49, 58–59
Brown & Brown Insurance, 99–100
Buffett, Warren, 70

Cain, Herman, 47
Caremark Pharmacy Services,
    38–39
Carson, Ben, 120
CVS Caremark Corporation, 38
Costa Rica, 30, 50, 55

Drucker, Peter, 40

eBay Inc., 53
Emery-Riddle Aeronautical
    University, 91–92
Experimental Aircraft Association,
    92

Ford Motor Company, 45
Ford, Henry, 45
Franchises, 47, 70
Franklin, Benjamin, 10

Gaston, A. A., 120
Giaudrone, Joe, 48
GoDaddy.com, LLC, 66
Godfather's Pizza, 47
Gore-Tex, 43
Gummi Bears, 60

Hal Riney & Partners, 76–79
Halkides, Mihalis, iv
Hallmark Gold Crown, 66
Hand, Russ, 79
Harley-Davidson Inc., 33, 40,
    50, 55
Harvard Business School, 20, 31
hhgregg, Inc., 66
Holland Financial, iv, 27, 40

Id Software, 92
Infogroup, Inc., 87, 92

InfoUSA, 87, 92
Instant Internet Empires, 24
International Business Machines
    Corporation (IBM), 47
Iocco, Robert, iii, 99–101

J. C. Penney Company, Inc., 52, 65
J. C. Penney's Beauty Salon, 89–91
Jesus, Christ, 105–106
Jobs, Steven, 62
Johnson, Ron, 60
Joseph LaBosco's Jewelry & Pawn,
    40

Kearns, Doris, 8
Kennedy, Joe, 79
Kern, Frank, 23–24
Kimberly-Clark Corporation, 43
Koch, Richard, iii

Layers of the 80/20 rule, 16–17,
    35–36, 46, 98, 101, 119
Lee, Richard, 47–48

Mallory, Dave, iii
Malaco, 60
MapWise Perceptual Mapping
    Software, 56
Marjorie's Rugs, 67
Mary Kay, 66
Myers-Briggs Type Indicator, 13

National Linen Service, 85–86
Newman, Mark E. J., 37
NeXT Inc., 62

Opportunity cost, 107

Pareto distribution, 14–16, 36–37
Pareto, Vilfredo, 5–7, 14–16, 36–37

Pendleton Condominium
    Association, 97–99
Penney, James Cash, 52
Pillsbury Company, 47
Pixar Animation Studios, 62
Porter, Michael, 20, 31
Pricing strategies, 57–58
Profitability, 39

Riley Technologies, LLC, 104
Riley, Bob, 104
Riney, Hal, 76–79
Robbins, Tony, 23–24, 121
Rogers, Will, 51
Romero, John, 92
Rooms To Go Incorporated, 63
Rumsfeld, Donald, 110

Saturn LLC, 59, 76–80
Schottky, Connie, iv
Sea-Doo, 48–49, 58–59
Seaman, Jeffrey, 63
Seaman's Furniture Company, 63
Soup to Nuts, 53
Swedish Fish, 60

Target Corporation, 60
Theory of comparative advantage,
    28–30
Thunderbird School of Global
    Management, 60
Trumpet, Juaquin, 17–18
Trustpoint Insurance, 100–101

W. L. Gore & Associates, Inc. 43
Wal-Mart Stores, Inc., 66

Do you want to order Aesop's Keys for friends?
Please go to *http://betsykruger.com/book/*

Thanks for your order.

CPSIA information can be obtained at www.ICGtesting.com
Printed in the USA
LVOW04s1833161114

413994LV00001B/1/P

9 781928 782582